'He honoured the past,
rejoiced in the present,
and
built for the future'

LONDON
VICTOR GOLLANCZ LTD
in association with
Peter Crawley
1986

Alec Clifton-Taylor's
BUILDINGS OF
DELIGHT

Edited by
DENIS MORIARTY

Design by Craig Dodd

© 1986 Estate of Alec Clifton-Taylor (Christopher Burkett); Denis Moriarty;
  Peter Crawley

British Library Cataloguing in Publication Data
Clifton-Taylor, Alec
   Alec Clifton-Taylor's Buildings of delight.
   1. Historic buildings —— England
   I. Title
   720'.942   NA961
   ISBN 0–575–03701–6

Printed in Great Britain by Jolly & Barber Ltd, Rugby, Warwickshire

Previous page: The Ley, Weobley

❧ CONTENTS ❧

PUBLISHERS' NOTE

*A*lec had selected his favourite buildings – all of them to be in England, to cover different building types and materials from all periods and from all parts of the country, and many to be not too well-known even if this meant forgoing some particularly dear to him. About thirty of the photographs had been taken and subjected to minute criticism – 'I really think those windows should have been *shut*' – followed immediately by something complimentary lest one felt too cast down. Suddenly, quite unexpectedly, he died and the book seemed still-born. Then I recalled Alec's saying early in our discussions that of all his books, this would be the easiest to write for what he wanted to say was already in his notes. My Gollancz colleagues felt that every effort should be made to complete the book and we were extremely fortunate in persuading Denis Moriarty, who produced *Six English Towns* for BBC tv and who had worked closely with Alec on the scripts, to undertake the editing of the notes. This he has done with consummate skill and judgement and we are greatly in his debt.

It had been intended to publish *Buildings of Delight* on Alec's eightieth birthday as a celebration. It is still a celebration of a wonderful man and, we hope, a memorial also.

I would like to use this opportunity to thank the National Trust, English Heritage and the many owners of the delightful buildings shown in this book for much kindness and help when taking the photographs.

PSC

December 1985

INTRODUCTION

*I*t was with the greatest of enthusiasm that I responded to Peter Crawley's request and encouragement to edit and complete Alec Clifton-Taylor's *Buildings of Delight*. I had the good fortune to produce the first two of his series of English Towns for BBC tv and to work with him over the last nine years of his life; we had formed a close partnership and warm friendship.

I was already aware of Alec's extraordinary inventory. He divided England into seven regions and then developed a carefully indexed system of detailed information and reactions to all the places he had visited over forty years, regularly updated and elaborately cross-referenced. These observations, noted with Alec's sharp eye for materials and colour, style and taste, were committed first to small exercise books, and then to specially prepared sheets of paper kept in envelopes and filed under each year's travels. These papers are the essence of this book, as they were for much of his previous published work. The notes varied in length and detail; I have tried to follow him where possible *verbatim* but where I have found the need to expand them or place them in a more easily understood context, I have turned first to Alec's other books, notably *The Pattern of English Building* and *English Parish Churches as Works of Art*. My next point of reference has been two works which he held in the highest regard as indispensable, and to which he told me he turned with pleasure nearly every day, namely Sir Nikolaus Pevsner's monumental series *Buildings of England*, and H. M. Colvin's *A Biographical Dictionary of British Architects*.

The task of doing justice in these pages to Alec has been a daunting but pleasurable one, and I hope that those who already know and love his work will enjoy an opportunity of reading him again, and those who are first-time readers will respond to his 'exercise in looking' which was his particular contribution to the study of architecture. I have tried within the constraints of one summer, the wide regional distribution of sites and a full-time job, to visit as many as possible of the buildings I did not know. Where I have quoted or followed authorities other than Alec, I have endeavoured to make due acknowledgement. I am conscious, too, of an enormous debt to the writings of many others unattributed whose works and opinions he would have consulted, as I have done. For any conspicuous omissions or serious errors in the text I must take sole responsibility.

I should like to express my sincere thanks for all the help I have received; first to Christopher Burkett (through the kindness of his father Philip) for so generously allowing access to the material, the copyright of which now resides with him; to all the owners, incumbents, curators and administrators of buildings who have shown such interest, answered queries and provided most useful guides; and to my employers, BBC tv, always enlightened and understanding, and who recognised in Alec the potential he was to deploy in the best Reithian principles of broadcasting – to educate, inform and entertain. I am grateful to Robert Storrar who read the text with keen eye for syntax and style, as he had done for some of Alec's previous books, and to Anne Jenkins who so efficiently and enthusiastically typed my manuscript. I wish particularly to thank Peter Crawley, not only for this opportunity, but also for his very original and perceptive photographs, all taken specially for this book. He, too, has been a kindly, encouraging, keen and critical publisher, and with his wife Joan, the provider of generous hospitality, as indeed have my old friends, James and Noreen Grout who offered me the quiet of their home in which to complete the book. I must thank also my family, Joshua, Edmund, Eleanor and Tristan for their welcome diversions and good humour, and most especially my wife Brigid for her support, particularly in taking up the domestic burdens between six and nine each morning when most of this book was written, before facing her own strenuous working day. Finally, but not least, I am forever grateful to my parents, Patrick and May, who first gave me the great love for England which Alec recognised and taught me to develop.

Denis Moriarty
London   January 1986

NOTE

In order to accommodate more conveniently Alec Clifton-Taylor's selection of locations in terms of balance and geographical spread, his inventory of seven regions of England has been reduced to six. Within this scheme his choice of buildings is described as far as possible in chronological order except where the production of the book has determined otherwise. A map reference accompanies each entry. This relates to the Ordnance Survey 1:50,000 first, second and Landrover series; first to the number of the sheet, and then a six-figure reference, eastings and northings in the usual prescribed manner.

Opposite: Broughton Castle

SOUTHERN ENGLAND

BUCKINGHAMSHIRE KENT LONDON OXFORDSHIRE SURREY SUSSEX

We begin with Romanesque. That is not to be dismissive of what went on in England before the Norman Conquest. There are of course important and interesting survivals from the Roman occupation, and the Saxon period – especially the 'basilica' at Brixworth in Northamptonshire, the crypt at Repton in Derbyshire, the sculptures at Daglingworth in the Gloucestershire Cotswolds, and the great tower at Earl's Barton in Northamptonshire, perhaps the only really beautiful example of pre-Conquest architecture in England. Works of art, however, really begin in earnest with the Normans. They built a great deal – castles, cathedrals, abbeys and churches, some enormous and ambitious, others quite humble, some austere, others decorated and alive with ornament. In truth, these are the earliest buildings of delight.

The church of St. Mary at Iffley, two miles south-east of Oxford is one. It was built about a hundred years after the Conquest and is large for a Norman church. It has a nave and chancel, though neither aisles nor transepts, and it is dominated by a massive central tower, all built in a warm-coloured yellowish limestone and roofed with stone slates. The west front is justly famous. The doorway is flanked by two blind arches of its own height, and it is rich in decoration set in three orders. The innermost is zigzag, a typical example of about 1170, and then there are two orders of beakhead. This is a motif of Scandinavian origin, similar to that at Reading Abbey, which is a little earlier, and at the church of St. Ebbe in the city of Oxford. Beakhead is a row of beast- or bird-heads – here there are nearly sixty on the outer arch and fifty on the inner, 'biting' into the moulding, and very sharp and ferocious they look. They have worn better at the arch than at the side. The dripstone, the outermost order, a hood mould which projects to throw off the rain, has the best carving. It is excellent; here are grotesques and signs of the Zodiac and the diligent can decipher the emblems of the Evangelists, a winged man for Matthew, a lion for Mark, a bull for Luke, and an eagle for John.

Above the doorway, the rose window is a Victorian restoration, and a most proper one. It is, indeed, an insertion and quite well done by J. C. Buckler 1856–7 who followed the line of a blocked round window of the twelfth century which had been replaced by a later one in Perpendicular style. It was one of a number of laudable Victorian efforts to restore the original design, for in the seventeenth century part of the gable had been destroyed when the roof was lowered and a parapet built. The three deeply recessed smaller windows above the rose, all equally profuse in zigzag and beakhead are therefore somewhat restored but not unsympathetically so. The small blind window with its lightly carved frieze below is entirely Victorian, not unattractive, but a figment of the imagination. Nonetheless this west front which was the entrance for ceremonial occasions is a great success and looks very fine. The usual way in was from the south, where the door, protected for a long time by a porch, has even more elaborate carving; rosettes, zigzag,

13

fantastic creatures, horsemen fighting, Samson with his lion, and a centaur suckling her young. It is well preserved; either the porch did its job extremely well or the hand of the restorer could not be resisted when the porch was removed in the early nineteenth century.

In the interior the nave is plain and quite unspoiled but the Victorian glass is poor and makes the church all too dark. The tower arches over the chancel, however, are tremendously rich. The Normans liked to make a show at the chancel arch, even in quite small village churches like Kilpeck in Herefordshire; here is the riot of zigzag again, two bands of deep-cut chevrons on the west side and an outer order of a large lotus-like flower on the side facing the congregation, and zigzag again on the other. Purbeck marble too makes an appearance in detached octagonal shafts which anticipate the Gothic style of the next century.

The sanctuary occupies the two bays east of the tower and the first bay has a Norman vault, in four parts with plenty of massive chevrons at the ribs, and a dragon's head for a boss. It looks much restored. To the east the progression is to Early English, vaulted again and much less heavy. It is altogether less complicated and there are beautifully simple sedilia of the same period. Just beyond the eastern arch of the tower which leads to the sanctuary, low down, at eye level or just below and fitted between the shafts is a joyous little carving, bursting with vitality: a bird rising from its nest. It is a delight.

St. Mary at Iffley was the gift of a wealthy patron, and what a gift! It is a wonderful example of a Romanesque church, complete and well preserved, without doubt one of the best Norman village churches in England.

Opposite: St. Mary, Iffley

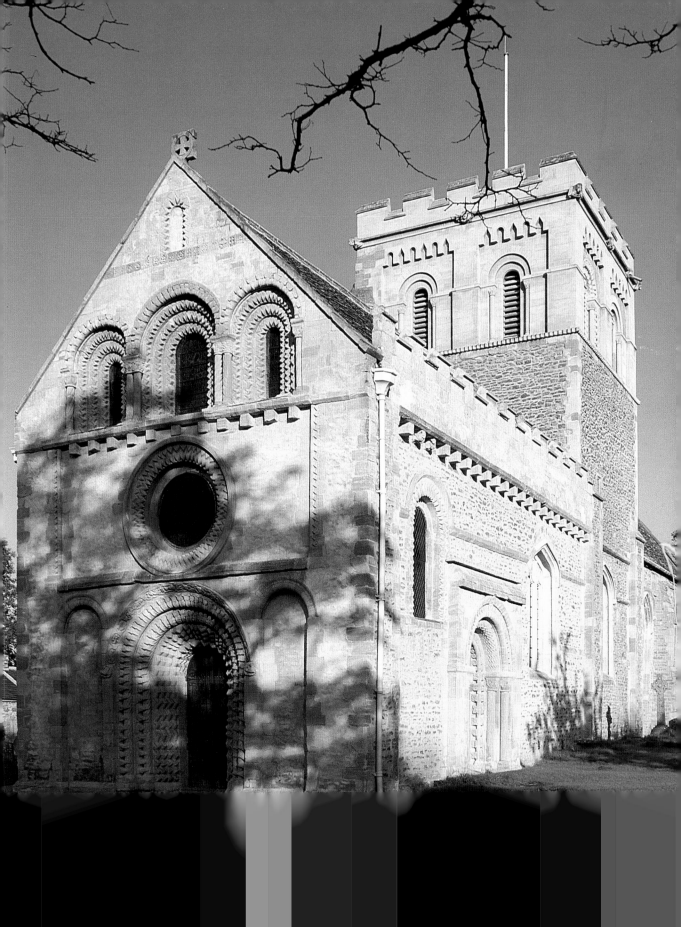

❧ BROUGHTON CASTLE

near Banbury, Oxfordshire   OS 151 418383

Oxfordshire wears a Janus face; in the south the chalk and flint of the Chilterns look to the Home Counties, and the commuters of Henley-on-Thames are only one hour from London; in the north the limestone announces the Midlands, Northampton, Warwick and beyond to Birmingham. This is the Marlstone region of the Midlands, and it yields an iron-tinted limestone rich in a variety of colours, and the best of all these stones was quarried at Hornton. Hornton is now, alas, no more, although a quarry very close to it is still dug at Edge Hill just across the Warwickshire border. It is this stone available only seven miles to the north that provides the material for Broughton Castle, the finest and most complete mediaeval house in the county.

The approach is from the north across a bridge guarded by a gatehouse, in the Decorated style, where a range of two-storey buildings now used as garages, shops, and the like, drops straight into the moat. This moat provides a spectacular setting; it is broad and goes the whole way round the house, at a good distance (save on the east side) which is lucky for the owners. It is pictorially a great asset. Broughton Castle was built in the fourteenth century as a fortified manor-house (not a castle designed solely for defence), and the fact that it is a house so evidently lived in and really a home adds much to the pleasure of a visit. It is the Fiennes family who have lived here for over five hundred years, and there is in the house the manuscript of the Journal of their seventeenth-century ancestor, Celia, the intrepid traveller and diarist who rode the length and breadth of England on her horse.

Licence to crenellate was granted in 1405; the fortified walls and parts of the gatehouse survive from this date. The oldest part of the house is the section to the east. It was built in 1306 and, following the normal domestic plan of that date, housed a first-floor solar and chapel over a vaulted undercroft. The large moulded three-light window of the chapel with its geometrical tracery can be clearly seen from the north-east. The lower building further to the east was a new kitchen built at the end of the sixteenth century. It was about that time that the whole of the north front (the main front) was reconstructed, and it is more or less symmetrical. The main door is not at all prominent, tucked away on the east bay, as at Burton Agnes in the East Riding of Yorkshire. As an ensemble the windows are now rather a hotchpotch, some having diamond panes, some rectangular leaded panes while a few even are Gothick, and are sashed with glazing bars.

Within there are many good things to savour; the Great Hall, Elizabethan, incorporating the original mediaeval house of 1300 and given a plaster ceiling with pendants in the 1760s; the Oak Room, loveliest in the house, lofty and light with a lot of attractive silvery oak, including a splendid interior porch with cartouche; and the main bedroom – Queen Anne of Denmark's bedroom, which has a peep-hole to the chapel. There are also a Long Gallery in the Gothick taste, a remarkably elaborate plaster ceiling in the Parlour above the Oak Room, and in the Star Chamber

Broughton Castle:
the gatehouse

16

an extraordinary chimney-piece, French, with a lower half of stone and a stucco overmantel. The dining-room (an undercroft of the mediaeval house) is venerable with a fine quadripartite ribbed vault and lovely linenfold panelling (wood carved to look like folds in carefully arranged fabric). Its date is about 1500, but sadly this room, already a little dark, faces north.

The great delight of Broughton Castle, apart from the wonderful setting, is the marvellous subtle colour of the stone; a delicate mixture of grey and gold and grey-green and golden-green. There is lichen on the walls in gentle 'blushes'. To complete the effect the roof is entirely covered with Stonesfield slates, carefully graded from bottom to top in the approved style. It is altogether a pleasure to behold.

✹ *LEEDS CASTLE*

Kent   OS 188 836533

'Wonderful in manifold glories' wrote Lord Conway, historian of castles 'are the great castle visions of Europe; Windsor from the Thames, Warwick or Ludlow from their riversides, Conway or Caernarvon from the sea, Amboise from the Loire, . . . Carcassonne, Falaise and Château Gaillard: beautiful as they are and crowned with praise they are not comparable in beauty with Leeds, beheld among the waters on an autumnal evening when the bracken is golden and there is a faint blue mist among the trees – the loveliest castle, as thus beheld, in the whole world.'

Words of praise indeed, and Lord Conway may well be right. The setting is superb; it is the lake that makes it, and to see this fairy-tale castle dropping sheer into its moat beautifully reflected in the water and set in a wonderful wooded rolling landscape is to be transported. Water surrounds the castle on every side, and it is joined to the 'mainland' by a bridge, and approached through a gatehouse. This leads to the outer bailey, a beautiful oval lawn laid out now and again for croquet, and looking especially lovely when the long shadows of early morning or late evening play upon it. To the right is the Maiden's Tower; in front is the castle façade and beyond it the gloriette, built upon a further island and linked by a two-storey stone bridge which in the early nineteenth century replaced the former one of timber.

The stone is the so-called Wealden stone, a sandstone which is to be found in central and eastern Sussex, and along the border with Kent. It has a fine grain and can be obtained in quite sizable blocks, and has a range of colour, fawns and greys, especially when enriched with a variety of lichen. It can look very good particularly when the sun is shining.

The building of the stone castle began in the early twelfth century and it has been much loved by its owners and residents over the centuries. For three hundred years it was a royal residence. It was a favourite home of Edward I and he it was who

made it over to his queen, Eleanor of Castile, as part of her dower, and thereby began a tradition that was to last over two centuries as an arrangement for no less than eight mediaeval queens, the last of whom was Catherine de Valois, queen to Henry V. The last private owner was Lady Baillie, who restored the gloriette, planted the wood garden, and imported exotic birds for the gardens and lake. After living here for nearly fifty years she bequeathed it to the Leeds Castle Foundation. The castle was opened to the public in 1976.

Much of the expansion and enrichment of the building dates from the reign of Henry VIII. He in effect changed Leeds Castle from a fort to a palace. He built the so-called Maiden's Tower for the royal maids of honour; it is rectangular with a later battlement (contemporary with the nineteenth century reworking of the main building) which hides a rather pretty red-tiled roof. He also had plasterwork and other improvements made to the main palace and from his time date the lovely bay windows which are the glory of the gloriette. The main part of the castle, and the bridge which joins it with the gloriette, however, are part of the programme of restoration and rebuilding carried out in about 1822. For some this is all an ordinary affair, unadventurous and straightforward, symmetrical and dull to a degree with its gatehouse, battlements and turrets, and yet it suits the site admirably. It is a very good neighbour, and consorts well with the rest of the building, and in no small way contributes to the feel of the mediaeval castle; it is Gothick doing a really good job.

Within all is spick and span and perhaps a trifle disappointing. Les Chambres de la Reine are unashamedly reconstructed and very 'repro', even to the point of a gas log-fire, while the real logs wait patiently in their basket, dressings for the set. However there are some good woodwork, a carved ceiling, some fine furniture, and two fireplaces, one in the Queen's Gallery carved in Kentish rag, the other in the drawing room with a splendid fireback, one of the earliest known in England. A sixteenth-century staircase, with a central twisted newel carved from a single trunk surmounted by a figure of a crusader, was imported here by Lady Baillie in the extensive rebuilding of 1926–8. The 'seminar room' has played host to many a prestigious conference and visits by foreign dignitaries, and it is hung with a modest but delightful collection of Impressionists – among them Boudin, Degas and Pissarro. The rooms are extremely well kept, and the route for visitors thoughtfully organised, a model of its kind.

The grounds are pure pleasure; five hundred acres of beautiful parkland around a lake, a golf-course, and even a duckery where waterfowl, rare geese and black swans cruise, and peacocks strut to their hearts' content. Everything, castle and grounds, is superb. Leeds Castle is, it must be said, one of the most expensive houses to see, but for its setting, and all it has to offer, it is worth every penny.

ABBOT'S HOSPITAL, GUILDFORD

Guildford is still, for all the degradations of the present century, a lovely town, and full of interest. It gains enormously from its setting, on slopes rising on either side of the valley of the River Wey as it cuts its course through the chalk of the North Downs and flows on to join the Thames. The steep streets that climb the hills give Guildford its character, and at the top of the High Street is Abbot's Hospital, an almshouse on which building began in the same year, 1619, as Sackville College in East Grinstead (p.26).

The Abbot in question, George Abbot, became Archbishop of Canterbury. He was one of three brothers, born locally and of modest beginnings who made good; one became Lord Mayor of London, and another the Bishop of Salisbury. Abbot's Hospital, built of a deep-red brick is a much more ambitious affair than its contemporary at East Grinstead. It was founded for twenty poor persons – the men were to outnumber the women by twelve to eight – and its frontage to the street certainly proclaims itself worthy of a Primate. The gateway, its single most prominent feature, is very grand. It rises to three storeys with large turrets at each of the four corners, ogee-shaped and lead-capped, with spirelets and pennants, more in keeping with the Tudor gatehouses of a Cambridge college or Hampton Court than a humble hospital.

To the right of the archway, to the east, lie the Master's Lodgings, and beyond the entrance a quadrangle, fifty feet or so square with three storeys, lodgings to either side and opposite the gateway a range with kitchen, dining hall and chapel. In appearance it is distinctly collegiate; mullioned windows and hand made tiles at the roof complete a largely unspoiled picture. The interiors and furnishings are likewise all of a piece. There is some splendid woodwork of the period, especially at the doors of the gatehouse, a little ponderous perhaps for some but obviously designed to impress. They have thirteen well carved panels, two of which bear the initials of its founder, and two his mitred coats of arms, with a monster fan light above, all set in a stone surround. In the Master's Lodgings there is an elaborate staircase with a narrow well and some good panelling, and elsewhere there are chairs and tables, even a bell, all contemporary with the foundation. Above the dining room is a banqueting hall and next door is the chapel with a Jacobean alms box and some Flemish glass in the windows, of moderate quality but complete and dated 1621, telling the story of Esau and Jacob.

Abbot's Hospital is a handsome endowment and an asset to the town; by any standards, for its architecture, comparative comfort and amenity, the founder did his poor persons proud. Its special pleasure lies in its brick and tile and carved woodwork; and its interest in that it survives almost entire as a fine example of the Jacobean almshouse – an outward manifestation of man's humanity to man.

Overleaf: Abbot's Hospital

SYNYARDS

Kent is very much the home of timber and tile, and just to the south-east of Maidstone, in the village of Otham stands a pleasing example of the Wealden house – Synyards, a confident personality glimpsed even by the casual passer-by along this increasingly suburban road. Closer to, it reveals itself as a late fifteenth-century house (or early sixteenth) with a gable added in 1663. It has, characteristically, a hall in the centre with a service wing to the right as you enter and a solar to balance it on the other side. The solar was the upper living-room of a mediaeval house and the word derives from the Latin *sol*, sun which, presumably, you hoped sometimes to enjoy even in the gloomiest of English summers. The two wings project from the centre with jetties, or overhangs, and this gives the hall its recessed effect. The Wealden house was designed to stand free as a farm house, but it may be found among other houses in town streets and indeed (like the Norfolk turkey and Aylesbury duckling) it turns up in areas well away from the Kentish Weald, for instance in Sussex and as far as Coventry and Oxford. But it is much more abundant in Kent than elsewhere, and Synyards, well kept, beautifully tiled throughout, sturdy and handsome, is a delight.

Opposite:
Abbot's Hospital

Below: Synyards

THE QUEEN'S COLLEGE LIBRARY

Everything of Robert of Eglesfield's college at Oxford founded in 1340 as The Queen's College, has disappeared. The Queen in question was Philippa to whom he was chaplain; the naming of his college was in part to get even with Edward III's King's Hall (later to become Trinity College at Cambridge) and partly the unlikely hope, cherished somewhat pedantically by those who insist on the 'The', that by such a distinction, future queens and consorts, not just his Philippa, would favour his establishment. Nowadays it is Queen's* as much as The Queen's, but the total loss of all the mediaeval buildings means that the college, of all the older foundations, has more stylistic unity than any other. It was all built within a hundred years, 1672–1765.

There is much to admire in the architecture. The showpiece must be the front quad, the finest classical example in Oxford, with its great screen on the High, its robust rustication, superb gatehouse and domed rotunda, and within, the wonderful colonnade to either side. The greatest treasure however lies in the west range of the earlier north quad. It is the Library built in about 1692–5. This is one of the glories of Oxford. It has eleven bays and at ground level was originally open to the quad (as was Wren's Trinity College library in Cambridge). This was filled in by C.R. Cockerell in 1841 to make more room for books. Each façade has a pediment, and the more ornamented elevation to the west which has a carved figure of Wisdom overlooks what is now the provost's garden. Within, upstairs, is perhaps the most gorgeous room in Oxford. It is glorious, and has a wonderful plaster ceiling, mainly the work of James Hands added to by Thomas Robarts some fifty years later. The effect, taken together with the layout of the library – superbly carved bookcases set at right angles to the windows in the usual way to provide bays – is quite breathtaking. At the southern end comes the climax: a brilliantly carved portal with figures of Art and Science on a broken segmental pediment and a coat of arms above. The craftsmanship is of the highest order. No library, not even Christ Church or the Codrington at All Souls can compare.

*Alec Clifton-Taylor was an undergraduate at Queen's from 1925–8 and loved Oxford and its architecture more, to be fair, than the pursuit of its history school. The library at Queen's was in his time somewhat musty, dirty, gloomy and forbidding. He was an occasional visitor, but only in recent years has its true splendour been revealed. Alec came to Oxford with a romantic love of Gothic, in particular the churches and cathedrals of England which were his chief delight. He was even somewhat dismissive of his own rather severe classical surroundings at Queen's, and much preferred the vault of Christ Church cathedral choir and the Divinity school (the work of William Orchard) and the Canterbury Quad at St. John's. Over the years his taste changed and he modified his view; he came to love Queen's best of all.

The architects and designers of Queen's College remain elusive. Wren was involved in the contract and design for the north quad, but it was much altered and the building lengthened and heightened in the eighteenth century. Hawksmoor, his pupil, is mentioned in connection with the screen and the gateway in the front quad but the rest of the design may have been by Dr. George Clarke of All Souls who succeeded Dean Aldrich as the leading light in Oxford architecture in the early part of the eighteenth century and is credited with Christ Church Library, built between 1717–38. Aldrich himself, Dean of Christ Church, Vice-Chancellor of the University from 1692 to 1695 and designer of the Peckwater Quad in his own college has been suggested for the library at Queen's.

Authentic hands are difficult to establish, but two members of the Townesend family, an extraordinary line of builders and masons who worked in Oxford on and

off during the eighteenth century were almost certainly involved. William Townesend was the most successful and important member of the family and is credited with much of the eighteenth-century *building* of Oxford; Peckwater at Christ Church, the Codrington at All Souls, the Fellows' building at Corpus, the north-east block of the garden quad at New College among them. But the work was to the design of others, and this perhaps was the case at Queen's where he *built* the front quad, hall and chapel to Dr. Clarke's designs and modified Hawksmoor at the screen and cupola. It is possible, however, that he was his own designer. In the Queen's College records he is referred to as 'architect' whereas his father, John, sometime Mayor of Oxford, and founder of the business, is merely credited with the title of stone mason. John was at the college from 1688 to 1712, and he may therefore have had a hand in the north quad. The line is difficult to draw, and the debate, fascinating to follow, will no doubt continue. The library, be it by Dean Aldrich or not, is wonderful, and its upper room, of its kind, something little short of a masterpiece.

SACKVILLE COLLEGE, EAST GRINSTEAD

Sussex   OS 187 398380

Despite an inner relief road on the site of a former railway cutting, East Grinstead is still too full of cars and roaring traffic, for essentially this should be a pleasing old market town with its excellent range of friendly domestic and public architecture. The best building, nicely placed on a little hill to the east of the parish church (rebuilt by James Wyatt in 1789), is Sackville College. It was built in 1619 as an almshouse for five men and six women (presumably a resident bachelor Warden would provide a balanced propriety). The benefactor was the second Earl of Dorset and he followed the familiar collegiate pattern of building the chapel, hall and dwellings around a courtyard. It has evidently been tinkered with a good deal (among others by Butterfield) but it is still entirely homely and attractive. Dr. J.M. Neale (1818–66) the great translator of hymns from the Early Church and himself the author of many – 'O happy band of pilgrims' to cite but one example – was Warden here for twenty years.

Sackville College is built of the local Wealden sandstone known to geologists as the Hastings beds (of sand and clay) and quarried in various places in central and eastern Sussex, especially near East Grinstead. It is the loveliest building stone in south-eastern England and the most reliable, a freestone of fine grain which yields a good ashlar. Sandstone too provides the material for the roof – slabs known generally as 'Horsham' slates, though they occur in many other places on the Wealden clay. With exposure they take on a quite pleasing grey-brown colour, but they are also very attractive to moss – picturesque maybe, but a danger to the rafters below and their weight needs massive support, provided here in the hall by a fine hammer-beam roof. The cupola has some pretty wooden shingles. While Sackville College may not perhaps be a major example of the almshouse, it is a very delightful building and, as it was intended, a haven from the busy world outside.

✿ CHAPEL OF ST. MICHAEL, RYCOTE

Oxfordshire   *OS 165 666047*

Opposite:
Chapel of St. Michael,
Rycote

The Chapel of St. Michael, Rycote, three miles south-west of Thame, is somewhat remote. It escapes the published collections of parish churches since it is the private chapel of the old manor house, now sadly no more, save for one red-brick typically Tudor tower, of 1539. The chapel, now in the care of English Heritage, is well worth seeing.

Outside, there is nothing very special. The chapel is built of Taynton stone with a red-tiled roof and good finials, and the tower, its most prominent feature, is a little stodgy. Since chapel and tower were built at the same time in 1449 and never altered, the building is historically important and has artistic unity. It is a happy foil to the notable interior, beautifully and very properly restored, with a lot of character and Archbishop Laud's feeling for Church and King. There are no aisles; the chancel and nave are as one, a delightful early setting for some later elaborate woodwork.

At the east end is the reredos of about 1700, with four fluted Corinthian columns, and carved with fruit and flowers – in the style of Grinling Gibbons. There are some pleasing altar rails of the turned baluster kind, and in the chancel, as in the nave, stalls with poppy-heads and pews with small buttresses which date from the original furnishings of the fifteenth-century church. It is the two 'fancy' pews, however, dating from the early seventeenth century, that are the focus of interest. The one at the north is traditionally known as the Norreys family pew. It has a ceiling painted with clouds and stars and above is a musicians' gallery with prettily carved panels somewhat Islamic in feeling. To the south, with its ogee 'dome' is the royal pew, erected, so it is said, for a visit to Rycote by Charles I in 1625. In its restoration the canopy has been beautifully painted with gold stars on a blue background, and the short black columns which support it are particularly handsome in black with gold relief at the capitals. It is all most colourful and successful.

Adjacent are an elaborate square Jacobean pulpit with a tester (a canopy serving as a sounding-board, presumably derivative from the French 'tête') and a later reading desk at a lower level. The wagon roof provides an admirable umbrella for these delights; it was originally painted blue with gold stars and a fragment has been wisely left to view at the west end. All this is best seen from the west gallery, seventeenth-century with Ionic columns, and the priest's room with its fire-place and floor above is certainly worth seeing, even if only for curiosity's sake!

✿ PITSTONE GREEN WINDMILL

Buckinghamshire   *OS 165 945157*

The approach to the windmill across a field from the B488 just a quarter mile south-east of Ivinghoe is anything but a delight. The backdrop is a large and ugly cement-works, a real blot on the landscape. But with back turned on the twentieth century, you are at once transported to the perfect prospect of a mill surrounded by wavy corn, and across the field the mediaeval spire of St. Mary, the village church, peeping through the beeches on gentle ridges of the Chiltern chalk just below Ivinghoe Beacon. Pitstone is a post-mill, rebuilt with timbers of an earlier mill some of which are dated 1627, which must make the mill one of the earliest anywhere in the country. This was before the invention of the fan tail (as at Saxtead in Suffolk, p.114) and in order to face the wind it had therefore to have to the rear a luff. This is in effect a rudder in the shape of a traditional pole with a wheel for easy manoeuvre. It was last in use in 1902 and restored from severe storm damage and disrepair by voluntary labour under the auspices of the National Trust in the 1960s. Its four fine sails, now at rest, were said to turn at fifteen revolutions per minute and to drive the two grindstones within at a hundred and twenty.

Overleaf:
Pitstone Green
Windmill

✿ KEW PALACE

Kew Palace, built in 1631 as a country house not far from the river, is now part of Kew Gardens (p.50). It is so by reason of its later acquisition as an annexe to Kew House. This was a royal residence now long since disappeared, whose grounds full of exotic plants were finally combined in 1802 with those of Richmond Lodge to form the nucleus of what today are the world-famous Botanic Gardens. Kew Palace, which stands now at one end of the Broad Walk, is the house to which George III repaired after he had lost his reason, and it was here that Queen Charlotte died in 1818.

It is an important and interesting essay in brick. It was built by Samuel Fortrey, a London merchant of Dutch origin. Because of his lineage and the gables to three sides with their double curves – the 'Dutch' motif of Amsterdam, later much

Opposite:
Pitstone Windmill

Below:
Kew Palace

favoured by Norman Shaw – it was for one hundred and fifty years or more known as the 'Dutch House'. These gables were not common in England at the time, nor was the style in which the bricks were laid. Instead of the traditional English bond – alternate courses of headers and stretchers – Flemish bond, alternate headers and stretchers in the same course, was employed.

There is more to Kew Palace than this. The bricks are more regular than those used previously, and this made for thinner joints in the mortar – a skill which reached fashionable peaks of refinement in the later Georgian age. Because the brick was also softer, it could more easily be rubbed down for more accurate jointing and for shaping and moulding in decorative devices, such as cornices, panels, pelmets and pilasters. This house is one of the earliest examples of such 'gauged' brickwork. Here on the south front it was used for rustication at the windows and keystones on the arches. But most spectacularly it can be seen at the superimposition of three architectural orders – Doric on either side of the door (the pilasters were unfortunately destroyed some years ago to make way for an ugly covered way which has quite deservedly in its turn suffered a similar fate), Corinthian at the first floor, cut correctly even to the point of the approved entasis, and Ionic above – quite a feat of carving!

It testifies more to skill than art, but there is much to enjoy at Kew Palace. It is very much of a piece and of its period. Moreover the craftsmen who built it were creating new possibilities in the use of brick. Kew Palace is one of the important landmarks in the history of English brickwork.

GROOMBRIDGE PLACE

Kent   *OS 188 533377*

Groombridge Place, three and a half miles west south-west of Tunbridge Wells, lies just by the border with Sussex, and its date makes it one of the most important survivors in Kent. It is a fine house built some time between 1652 and 1674 within the courtyard of an earlier mediaeval house which explains the moat, very wide in proportion to the 'new' house, and the stables to the south that stand within it. The rebuilding was undertaken by Philip Packer (whose father John had bought the house from the Wallers in 1618) and he is somewhat unhappily commemorated in a monument of odd invention, half-naked and lolling, by John Bushnell in the nearby parish church.

The house is a delight and marvellously kept. It is built on the H-plan, only one room thick, with a hall and chamber above at the crossbar of the H, and it connects stylistically with other houses in West Kent of the same period at Chevening Park and Yotes Court near Mereworth. It is built of red brick (brick quoins too) mostly in the Flemish bond – courses laid with alternating headers and stretchers. All this is offset with sandstone dressings at the windows and a colonnade, or loggia, with Ionic columns surmounted by a pediment. This serves in effect as a porch in the middle of the house and hides its two front doors. The woodwork here and at the windows is painted buff to match the stone, and this detracts somewhat from the impact of the west front. White is certainly to be preferred – even for the stone of the colonnade – for the contrast with the beautiful mellow colour of the brick would then be seen to much greater effect.

The windows were originally casements, and the present sashes, almost the only significant alteration to the exterior since its building, have glazing bars, four across and six up, which make for somewhat square proportions. The chimney stacks, with lofty sunk panels, project from the bays, and their pots which once looked like triangulation points have now happily been replaced by those of a more conventional kind. Within there are some re-worked fittings from the earlier house, linenfold panelling and a delightful plaster ceiling, but the real joy of this house lies in its dark red roofs, the variety of texture and lovely hand made tiles. The dormers too (here with diamond panes) are very pretty. Beautiful gardens rise in terraces to the north of the house. What a home!

Below:
Groombridge Place

T his design of Chicheley Hall is now known to be by Francis Smith, the Smith 'of Warwick' who worked at Ditchley Park (p.39), and whose practice included a number of major country houses in the Midlands. He was the son of a brickmaker, and from these humble origins he rose from being a stone mason to become one of the master builders of English architecture. He was twice Mayor of Warwick, where he is somewhat unflatteringly commemorated in a portrait which hangs in the Council Chamber. He was no genius, but he left a collection of handsome and original buildings to his name.

Chicheley Hall, two miles north-east of Newport Pagnell, was completed between 1719 and 1721. It is built in a lovely red brick with dressings of stone from the famous Weldon quarry in Northamptonshire. The house stands in beautifully maintained gardens, and is in the ownership of the Beatty family who keep it, as befits their tradition, in excellent shipshape order.

The south front is the stylish one, of a striking and decidedly original design. The most interesting feature, and characteristic of Smith, is at the centre, where the design 'sweeps forward'. But in reality the projection is comparatively tiny, and the effect much bolder than it actually is; there is a touch of theatre here, and how successful it is! The giant Corinthian pilasters, the finely-carved frieze (an admirable adornment above the three centre first-floor windows), and the unusual heads to the architraves of these windows at both first- and second-floor storeys, all combine to give this elevation much character. The projection is further differentiated by the use of round-headed windows. There are perhaps two defects; the door which has an unfamiliar frame is too small and lacks sculpture above, but more seriously the roof-line is cut off too abruptly, and at this level the absence of parapet and cornice is keenly felt.

The house is regularly open to the public and there are some fine features within. The entrance hall is a delight, two storeys high, with a marble floor and an unusual triple arch, also in marble, which on the inner side provides a link to a spacious and beautiful staircase. This is made of oak inlaid with walnut and each tread has a trio of balusters, a small spiral, a flute and a big corkscrew, with carved brackets under the stair ends. It is of splendid proportions, very refined, and almost delicate. In other rooms there is much bold decoration of the period; pilasters, panelling, cornices and handsome plasterwork and a number of good doorcases and fireplaces.

Many of the windows preserve their original hand made crown glass with its lovely glinting reflections. This is often contained within glazing bars, which are flat, broad and contemporary with the house, while the thinner ones reveal a later date. On the east side of the house there are some good rainwater heads and original down pipes. But perhaps the greatest joy of all is the brickwork; ordinary Georgian brick but of a rich orange-red with quite a number of blue headers. In the centre, the *piano nobile* is faced with small rubbers, very finely jointed. Brick was not used as the principal material at Chicheley Hall because it was cheap; on the contrary, it was chosen for its quality and with a purpose so that the colours might set off the whiteness of the stone, and moreover that the smallness of the bricks might by comparison give greater effect to the scale of the pilasters and a pleasing texture to the surface of the walls. It does so with considerable success; the effect is quite remarkable.

Below:
Chicheley Hall

✤ ST. PETER, GAYHURST

'A wretched building showing much eighteenth-century rubbish' wrote E.S. Roscoe in 1903; 'one of the classical-style treasures of the country' was the verdict of John Betjeman and John Piper half a century later, and how right they were. The church, approached along a lane through beautiful parkland with grazing cattle, was begun in 1728, a complete rebuilding of the mediaeval church which had stood in the grounds of the great Elizabethan house nearby. The church is of course always accessible, and visitors should not be deterred by too many fussy little notices proclaiming the privacy of the neighbouring houses.

No expense was spared. It is built of a rather yellow limestone, from Ancaster perhaps or Weldon, ashlared throughout and with much rustication at the quoins and plinths, and Ionic pilasters and columns at the nave. There are pediments to the south and north (a double one indeed), and a niche instead of a window at the east end. The tower is less successful; despite its graceful tall pilasters it is marred by the perhaps later introduction of tracery to the windows. It does not seem quite to belong, despite the fanciful little cupola, made of lead, on top.

Within there is much to admire, and a lot of light in which to see it streaming in through eight plain round-headed windows with leaded lights, most of them having their original glazing. The absence of stained glass is lucky, and absolutely right. The walls, all of limestone, are now most subtly and lightly limewashed, in an off-white stone colour at the nave with architectural details in pale biscuit relief, and a pale grey at the chancel walls and nave arch. It is all very unobtrusive and successful. There is much else by way of excellent restoration; beautiful and elaborate white plaster ceilings, the 'Wrenish' reredos renewed, and the exquisite wrought-iron communion rails painted a dark blue-grey with details picked out and gilded. There are box pews (regrettably one section of the nave contains inappropriate chairs) and a two-decker pulpit. The pulpit proper is raised aloft with a spectacular sounding-board overhead; it is a real whopper, with marquetry on the underside, and quite grand. The Victorian font, a horrid intrusion and quite wrong here, is happily no longer in evidence, and a tiny font, on polygonal pillars contemporary with the church is in its place.

Gayhurst is not strong on inscriptions. At the reredos there is a double negative in the first of the Ten Commandments; 'Thou shalt not have none other Gods but Me,' and at the monument, baroque and prominent in the nave, there is no inscription at all. It is to Sir Nathan Wright, Keeper of the Great Seal, and his son George, two life-size figures in long wigs, white marble against grey marble. At first this monument might appear rather provincial, but there is real life in both their figures, and it is outstandingly good. It is *not* however by Roubiliac, neither is the church, as was once surmised, by Wren. Even without this roll call, this is a delightful church, entire in itself, stylish and distinguished.

DITCHLEY PARK

Five and a half miles north-west of Woodstock stands Ditchley Park, third in size and date of Oxfordshire's grand eighteenth-century mansions.

It is built to the Palladian plan of a centre and wings and replaced an earlier timber building. Ditchley Park was begun about 1720 and engaged the minds and talents of the same brilliant team of designers and decorators which had just completed the short-lived Canons in Middlesex. The architect was James Gibbs (though much of the building seems to have been left to Francis Smith 'of Warwick') in collaboration with William Kent.

The scheme is best appreciated from the south-east, a grand elevation of eleven bays with quadrant colonnades, now glazed, linking the house to a pair of side wings, each of seven bays and sizeable enough houses in their own right. They are surmounted by pretty cupolas both rising above handsome black and gold clocks. All this is built of beautiful buff-coloured Taynton limestone. The masonry is superfine; the joints almost invisible from a hundred feet away.

Opposite:
St. Peter, Gayhurst

Below:
Ditchley Park

The windows, somewhat square for some tastes, are all sashed and painted white, six by three at the *piano nobile*, the first floor of the main house, and three by three at the attic which rises above a bold cornice. But at the side wings the windows are six by four below and four by four above, with smaller lights. Quite a times-table for the arithmetically aware! The wings oddly enough have grey slate roofs, not at all right here, and strange indeed when you consider Stonesfield stone slates were available only two and a half miles away.

The skyline is very jolly with urns and vases and on this south-east front are two lead figures; Fame, with a trumpet, and Loyalty, the work of Carpentière* (who made similar figures for Canons) about 1730. The railings which enclose the court-yard are of a pleasing light design and look like cast iron of about 1830 and there are a charming lantern and double gates, again cast iron, on stone bases.

Within, there is a lot to see. The entrance hall, a cube or very nearly so, is a rich and splendid room with fine doorcases, chimney-pieces and furnishings mainly by Kent, all set off by the lively stucco of the Italians Artari, Serena and Vassali. Henry Flitcroft was also at work here between 1736 and 1741. Some patron, this George Lee, second Earl of Lichfield! In the Tapestry Room there is a pretty chimneypiece of white marble, adorned with carvings of fruit and a central mask; and in this room, as elsewhere, there are much in evidence nicely moulded shutters and tremendously thick glazing bars pointing to an early date. The Velvet Room, with a design of the Hindu god Shiva, is hung with Genoese velvet, crimson and gold, and very pleasing too. The White Room shows an Adam influence especially in the partly gilded ceiling, which does not really suit this house, but here are another handsome white marble chimney-piece and two fantastic eagle tables by Kent. Beautiful furniture abounds and there are numerous bedrooms, all admirably furnished and luxurious. The staircase, the handrails at least of oak, is not at all grand but is prettily carved. The Saloon, at the centre of the house overlooking the garden, reveals the Italian *stuccatori* in full flight, with a lot of pleasant sculptures, fluent and competent though not highly pleasurable and the lack of pictures makes this one of the least enjoyable rooms. But make no mistake; overall this house has some sumptuous interiors.

The Garden front overlooks a perfect formal garden with box designs, prelude to a large lawn flanked by avenues of lime, and a grand avenue in the park. Beyond Lancelot 'Capability' Brown's lake, formed and landscaped in 1770, is a *tempietto*, circular and rather large, and quite an eye-catcher from the house. It is of rubble-stone, cement rendered but the surface is not unpleasant, and it has a coffered 'pantheon' dome.

Ditchley Park has no pediment, no pilasters, no other adornments nor even (at the centre) a visible roof. There are no subtleties and some may even find the pavilions a little too large. It may not therefore be a work of genius, but it is highly accomplished; and it is in excellent hands and exquisitely kept.

*Andries Carpentière, c.1670–1737, who anglicised his name to Andrew Carpenter shortly after his arrival to work in England.

RADCLIFFE OBSERVATORY

For some, the Radcliffe Observatory is the loveliest building in Oxford; for Nikolaus Pevsner* it is 'architecturally the finest observatory in Europe'. It is, as the name implies, one of the major benefactions of John Radcliffe (1652–1714) an Oxford medical graduate and physician to Queen Anne. He gave money for a library housed in the Radcliffe Camera, for travelling fellowships in medicine, and for the Infirmary and the Observatory.

Facilities for studying the heavens in early eighteenth-century Oxford were of little account. Observatories were confined to rooms high up in the Bodleian, at Corpus Christi College, and in a house in New College Lane, where from his personal observatory Halley predicted the return of his comet, which turned up in 1758, later than he had forecast. The Radcliffe Observatory, which occupies a site off the Woodstock Road adjoining the Infirmary, was begun in 1772 to designs by Henry Keene who was surveyor to Westminster Abbey and architect at Worcester College. He died and the work was completed in 1794 to a different design by James Wyatt, the leading architect of his day.

It is a noble building, original and exciting in conception, confident and marvellous in execution, and its fine ashlar limestone looks very good indeed in its recent restoration. The main façade is to the south but the rear – which now has the entrance across a pleasant lawn – is just as good. Of the fifteen bays, five to the left, and five to the right (which are linked to the Observer's house by corridor) are of only one storey. In the middle of the Observatory fluted columns provide a handsome doorway; then at the first floor, the *piano nobile*, are more pilasters, and above the lovely tall windows signs of the Zodiac and a balustrade. Then Wyatt produced his *coup de théâtre*, a version of the 'Tower of the Winds', an irregular octagon with one long side with pediment front and back and short diagonal sides for the other six. All the sides have large windows and tall columns and are decorated with architectural sculptures of the winds, and the tower is topped by the figures of Hercules and Atlas holding a globe in copper – all the work of the sculptor John Bacon.

Three rooms inside, one on top of the other, follow the shape of the exterior with some good plaster work, and solid-looking doors. They are reached by a lovely swirling staircase set in a semi-circular extension to the north and lit from the top by a dome. Even the lavatory door at the entrance follows the line of the curve! Not much of the furniture designed by Wyatt survives except for a pair of mahogany desks, some telescope steps and a set of chairs. Some of the instruments, ordered from a famous maker, Bird, were larger than those at Greenwich, and the eighty-four inch telescope, the largest ever built in Europe save one (by the same maker for the King of Spain) was removed in 1935 to South Africa. Oxford was never, in astronomical terms, an ideal place for gazing at the stars, although the weather is still studied, as it has been since 1767 when Dr. Hornsby set up his meteorological

investigations, and solar observations are made from domes in the university parks. The Observatory and its instruments celestially speaking are no more** but architecturally it is the centrepiece – indeed the showpiece – of Green College, founded in 1977 to cater for clinical medical students and their teachers, and Wyatt's fine creation provides lecture and common-room facilities for members of the college. It was originally sited to form the focal point of both St. John's and Walton Streets, but the vista was ruined by the erection of Wellington Square, and the ruin was compounded more recently by the building of the Nuffield hospital. Isolated as it is, it remains a fine monument to the study of the 'spangled firmament on high', and it is good to see it so beautifully restored and put to such good use.

*The Buildings of England: Oxfordshire, Jennifer Sherwood and Nikolaus Pevsner, Penguin 1974.

**Until its change of use, at the start of each Michaelmas term the University Gazette carried this notice: 'The Director of the University Observatory gives notice that on fine and clear Thursday evenings in the Michaelmas and Hilary terms between 8 and 10 p.m. celestial objects will be shown through the telescope to members of the University and friends accompanying them'.

❀ SOMERSET HOUSE

London   *OS 176 307808*

From whichever direction you approach, Somerset House reveals an imposing and perhaps even forbidding presence. It is obviously a building of some public importance; indeed it was so, and happily in the recent restoration of the Fine Rooms within, it still is. It enjoys a commanding site in the Strand, bounded by the River Thames to the south, and the northern approach to Waterloo Bridge to the west.

Sir William Chambers was Surveyor General to the King, and the leading architect of his day, and his building epitomises much the same attitude to the culture of the establishment as Sir George Gilbert Scott's Whitehall was to official taste a hundred years later. Somerset House was built to house a whole range of government departments – the Privy Seal, the Exchequer and Audit, the Navy, the Duchy of Cornwall to name but four – and also the three learned societies under royal patronage: the Royal Society, the Society of Antiquaries and the Royal Academy of Art.

The river front is the most dramatic and was obviously intended to outshine the Adam Brothers' recent Adelphi just downstream river. It has two storeys, for the site was on a slope down to the river, and the lower with its massive arches and river entrance flanked by huge columns would have been lapped by the Thames until just over a century ago. Above is a terrace, now eight hundred feet long, with its nineteenth-century extensions to east and west, which in no way impinge on Chambers's composition. It has many strong points: a lot of rustication, lofty pilasters crowned with finely carved capitals, a recessed centre portico and pediment and a handsome balustrade. The most unusual feature perhaps is the arch, a complete semi-circle which gave access to the courtyards beyond. It is all very elegant and self-assured, classicism beyond reproach.

Somerset House is built, or at least faced throughout with Portland stone, except in some of the side courts where the more workaday brick sufficed. Portland stone, the 'king of the oolite' with its close grain and even texture – too urbane for some – is arguably the finest building stone in England. It withstands weather and pollution better than most, and when washed by the rain gleams white in the sun. It is particularly suitable for whole buildings, and ones that must announce dignity and nobility. What a shining example it projects across the river to the concrete of the South Bank, which so quickly becomes blotched and stained. What a missed opportunity! London is surely worthy of the very best.

✤ CUMBERLAND TERRACE

Regent's Park, London   OS 176 287833

*I*n the early years of the nineteenth century, John Nash emerged as the leading architect of the 'picturesque', and brought the garden city to London. He produced a whole scheme for Regent's Park, villas scattered in shady groves with a backdrop of trees, crescents and terraces. Not all of his plan came to fruition, but much did, and Cumberland Terrace, built in 1826 and one of the terraces which surround two-thirds of the park, is perhaps the most spectacular and successful of his designs. It is on a grand scale; eight hundred feet long, with a projecting centre block, ten giant Ionic columns, cornice, balustrade, and a pediment alive with sculpture.

Nash's conceit was entirely English; no imitation ever appeared on the continent. Clearly he most ingeniously understood the partiality the English have for life in the town as well as in the country away from the town. This is indeed *urbs in rure* as well as *rus in urbe*. It is all, of course, a bit of a show; these imposing palatial façades are pure sham, for behind lurk ordinary brickwork and very ordinary houses. Pretention on such a scale and at an economic price (for therein lay the key) was made possible by the use of stucco – a hard external finish embodying some form of cement with the intention of imitating stonework, and the extent of stucco was much aided by the appearance of a number of patent external renderings which became available in the first twenty years of the nineteenth century.

The most important of those renderings was Parker's Roman cement, made in Harwich, which had great strength, durability, and could withstand damp. It is said to have been the mainstay of Nash's achievements. As a condition of the leases at Regent's Park (the leasehold of the old Marylebone Park had in 1811 reverted to the Crown) the terraces had to be repainted and the stucco's colour wash renewed every four years always in the imitation of Bath stone, and the Crown Commissioners still impose repainting of all the terraces at this interval, between the months of June and September and 'at no other time'. Oil paint, unknown in Nash's day, and introduced to London in about 1840, makes an ideal substance – the smoother and glossier the better – and while this heavy paint on stucco means no-one now would be deceived into thinking Cumberland Terrace is anything but what it is, it does provide a most handsome and resplendent livery.

Stucco has always had its critics. The Victorians disliked it on moral grounds; it was dishonest. For Sir John Summerson it is 'in a sense a fake material'; for Mr. John Harvey 'a poor thing'. Sir Nikolaus Pevsner thought that the conversion of some of these 'make-believe palaces' to government offices a telling sign of the times and 'most fitting for buildings of this size and character'. Be that as it may, Cumberland Terrace, all spruced up as it is today, glimpsed through the verdant green of the park and gleaming in the afternoon sun, wears a smiling face, well-mannered, light-hearted and urbane, the country mansion come to town.

Above and left:
Cumberland Terrace

BALCOMBE VIADUCT

Sussex   *OS 198 323278*

Travel by the fast electric train from Victoria to Brighton, and you will certainly miss one of the railway sights of the south-east – the Balcombe Viaduct, spanning the Ouse just south of Crawley. It is 1,475 feet long and was completed in 1841. The engineer was John Urpeth Rastrick.

Its span is well seen from the Haywards Heath road, a quarter of a mile to the east. The balustrade, classical in inspiration, is made of Caen limestone brought from Normandy, and it provides a delightful foil to the arches which are almost entirely of brick. At each end of the balustrade, the special feature of this design (scarcely glimpsed in any illustration which must of course concern itself with the width and span) are four aedicules, purely ornamental in intention, and probably, like the balustrade itself, the work of David Mocatta.* He was architect for several buildings on the London to Brighton line including the present frontage of the main Brighton station.

The piers, delicately tapering and splayed, give real pleasure to the eye. But the most unusual and perhaps most rewarding view – if you are prepared to risk muddy shoes and the stinging nettles – is from beneath, by the banks of the Ouse, with the extraordinary if not unique perspective through the arches which appear to recede almost to infinity.

The brickwork is mostly dark, patched somewhat clumsily here and there in pink. This viaduct would be still finer had it been entirely built in stone, but in this part of the world that would have been a real extravagance. Even so, it undoubtedly makes a most impressive contribution to the landscape.

*I am indebted for this information to R.T. Horne, Deputy Regional Architect, British Railways Board – Editor.

49

PALM HOUSE, KEW GARDENS

Surrey

Lilac time, any time, many times, and oh so near to London! The botanic gardens at Kew are unsurpassed anywhere in the world. There were two great formative periods in their history; in 1750 Sir William Chambers assumed responsibility for their initial layout and development and built the Orangery and Pagoda. A hundred years later Sir William and Sir Joseph Hooker in turn extended and increased the area sevenfold to seventy-six acres. It now numbers nearly three hundred. From Sir William Hooker's time dates the Palm House, a building of great beauty and wonder, a constant source of uplift, surprise and delight. It was built in 1844–8, 'one of the boldest pieces of nineteenth century functionalism' as *The Buildings of England** has it, 'much bolder indeed and hence aesthetically more satisfying than the Crystal Palace ever was'. It is a most exciting space, three hundred and sixty-two feet long, twenty-three feet high at its wings and rising in a giant but gentle quasi-ogee curve to sixty-two feet at the centre.

Its inspiration was perhaps Paxton's Great Stove – the huge conservatory at Chatsworth, now unfortunately destroyed, but that had wooden ribs for the frame. Here all is cast iron and glass, materials indeed of their time and used to glorious effect. It is at once robust yet delicate, strong in personality, yet blithe in spirit. It is like 'some fabulous object' wrote Olive Cook** 'or a transparent dome moored like a balloon to its base' in a sea of green. Aesthetically it gains enormously from its succession of identical curves; to step inside is to enter another world, a wonderful space, exotic greenery, sticky tropical heat. The engineer who designed it was Reginald Turner of Dublin and the architect was Decimus Burton – their Palm House is somewhere to visit again and again.

The Buildings of England: Surrey, Ian Nairn and Nikolaus Pevsner, rev. Bridget Cherry, Penguin, 1971, p. 327.
**England:* notes on Edwin Smith's photographs, introduced by Angus Wilson, Thames and Hudson 1971, p. 203.

NORTHERN ENGLAND

CHESHIRE CUMBERLAND DURHAM LANCASHIRE NORTHUMBERLAND YORKSHIRE

Previous page: Warkworth Castle

❧ LANERCOST PRIORY

Cumberland

OS 86 556638

Lanercost has a most beautiful situation, three miles north-east of Brampton in that marvellous stretch of country between Newcastle and Carlisle crossed by the Emperor Hadrian's spectacular Wall. The approach is across a delightful mediaeval bridge over the River Irthing, and the grounds are entered by a Norman gateway. It was a priory for Augustinian canons begun in the middle of the twelfth century, and despite damage done by marauding Scots in the two centuries that followed, and the later Dissolution, much of the church survives. It is built of at least two different kinds of stone, readily available locally although probably not hewn specially but taken from the Roman Wall which passes less than a mile to the north.

The west front, and a fair amount of the exterior besides, is entirely of pink sandstone. This front is a singularly chaste composition in lancets and frieze arcading above a rather elaborate door. High up in the gable there is a well-preserved sculpture of St. Mary Magdalene, mantle raised over one arm, and quite a familiar image of the mid-thirteenth century. There is an aisle to the north, but not to the south, for here ran the cloister. The aisle and nave now comprise the parish church.

Inside, the stone of the nave is a great surprise; no pink at all in evidence, for now it is all a grey-buff limestone, and for some of the internal piers yet another stone, yellower and different again. The nave is extremely lofty and has a wagon roof. Its chief delight is the clerestory, a gorgeous affair on both sides, with outsize 'dog-tooth', a fine sight. The stained glass, Morris and Co. and ascribed to Burne-Jones, is fortunately not very prominent.* The remainder of the building, the ruinous part, is now in the care of English Heritage. It is, as usual, very well maintained. The most important feature is the eastern part of the church, complete with aisles, transepts, and even a section of ribbed vaulting on the east side of the north transept and north side of the choir. This is Early English at its most beautiful, and herein are several large tombs of the Dacre family to whom the buildings were transferred at the Dissolution in 1536. There is still quite a lot to be seen, including a somewhat plain central tower, rising to a level just above the gable of the transepts.

The cloisters were rather small, but buildings survive to the west and south. Here is the undercroft, sturdy, impressive, and quite complete, which contains some interesting Roman altars and tombstones. To the west the restored building has been given a roof and is now put to excellent use as a village hall. Adjacent lies a house, rambling and romantic, a building of the sixteenth or early-seventeenth century where Sir Thomas Dacre first took up residence. It is still very much a home, and to the south is a pele tower, or a keep, formerly the prior's lodging.

Lanercost is a lovely place, the architectural gem of the diocese of Carlisle.

*Alec Clifton-Taylor was not a great admirer of the pre-Raphaelites! Many might disagree about these windows – Editor.

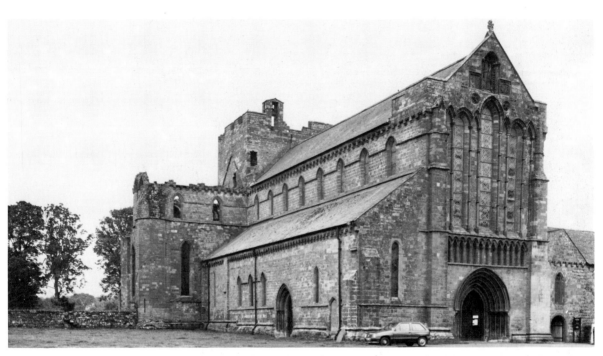

Opposite, top,
Lanercost Priory:
bottom, the
Cellarium (undercroft)

Left, South Transept
and Choir

55

RIEVAULX ABBEY

The ruins of Rievaulx Abbey are a beautiful and romantic sight, best seen in the early morning or late afternoon in spring or autumn, well away from crowds. For the Cistercians who built this marvellous Abbey, more of which survives than at any other monastic site in England save Fountains, loved a lonely spot, wild and remote. It had, of course, too, to have a good water supply, and here it was, in the valley of the River Rye (Rye *vallis* hence Rievaulx) twenty or so miles north of York, on its way south from the Cleveland Hills to the Derwent and then on to drain into the sea at Kingston-upon-Hull. There was also good stone available, only three miles down-river at Hollin Hill (opposite Duncombe Park). It is a Jurassic sandstone, lightish-brown in colour, fine in texture, and similar seams were to go on down the centuries making great contributions to English architecture; most of Castle Howard was built of it, and it provided the facing for Walpole's great house at Houghton.

The Cistercians came, as the name implies, from Cîteaux in Burgundy. They were Benedictines, but a reforming order, following a more austere and what they considered most authentic interpretation of the rule. Between 1128 and 1150 they built no fewer than thirty-five houses in England, and no Cistercian building in France survives earlier than Rievaulx or Fountains in the West Riding. The ascetic taste of the Cistercians led them to disapprove of decoration, and it was perhaps this that left them more open to functional invention – the pointed arch (introduced at Rievaulx in 1131), the flying buttress, and rib vault, all of which became the hallmark of Gothic architecture. This made too for light, height and proportion.

In its heyday, it was said that Rievaulx housed something like one hundred and forty monks and six hundred lay brethren and when the building reached its climax between 1225 and 1240 it must have been a superb sight. There is still much to see. The church, unusually for a mediaeval church, was built on a north–south orientation presumably to accommodate the site for such a large foundation between hill and river. It is particularly fine, as indeed is the refectory which has a noble height and dignity. There is also much enjoyment to be derived merely from plotting the monastic layout, from cloister to chapter house, library to sacristy, parlatorium to treasury, warming house to lavatorium, kitchen to infirmary. Be sure to take your Pevsner if you want to play the architectural detective: a richly rewarding pursuit and of the greatest interest, or why not for once leave aside the double-chamfers, quatrefoils, fillets and scallops and just delight in this most evocative and picturesque of pleasures? Rievaulx is glorious, a feast for the eyes, and without a doubt the finest of our ruined abbeys.

Opposite: Rievaulx Abbey

❧ SELBY ABBEY

West Riding of Yorkshire

Selby was always a place on the way to somewhere else; a queue at the toll-bridge on the old winding road north to York, or a windy platform when changing trains between the two long straight stretches of rail between Doncaster and Kingston-upon-Hull. From both situations the abbey church of St. Mary loomed; it could not, and it should not, be missed. It is immense!

Selby was a Benedictine abbey and it is rare therefore for such a church to have survived the Dissolution without becoming a cathedral, like Gloucester, or a focus of national importance such as Westminster. For Selby is now a parish church, in company with six other outstanding former monastic churches; Tewkesbury, Bath (also the seat of a bishop), Sherborne and Romsey – all Benedictine too, and Great Malvern and Christchurch, both priories. Only two other parish churches have three towers, Melbourne in Derbyshire and Beverley Minster; for today's towns, parish churches of this size must present a great problem to maintain.

Building began about 1100 and was to continue for over two hundred years; overall the length of the church now extends to about three hundred feet. There have been two disasters; in 1690 the central tower collapsed, not so unusual in a mediaeval church, and crashed onto the south transept, and in 1906 the whole church was damaged by a terrible fire. The earlier restoration and rebuilding of Sir George Gilbert Scott in the last thirty years of the last century, had to be undertaken again. His son J. Oldrid Scott was the architect. The crossing tower was again rebuilt and the west towers finished, and only for the first time, in 1935. So the exterior of the church in some respects wears quite a Victorian air; it is well executed but only moderately satisfactory. The detailing, for example, at the central tower is very good, but as a whole it lacks authority and the west towers, for all their ingenuity, are decidedly too short.

The north door, however, is extremely fine. It has plenty of zigzag and geometrical ornament and is of the same Norman period of building as the west portal. At the choir there are some delightful crocketed buttresses, and the east window, together with that at Carlisle, is among the best examples of the flowing Decorated style in the country. The tracery, adorned with many cusps, is certainly very pretty although perhaps a little thin and too complicated for some who might prefer the more robust examples, such as at Higham Ferrers. About half of its stained glass is fourteenth-century and contemporary with the window.

Inside, the nave is huge. It is a pity that the ubiquitous Victorian glass in every window makes it far too dark. The nave was built in the twelfth and thirteenth centuries and it provides a rewarding exercise if one tries to read dates and development. There are massive round piers, one with diapers as at Durham, then some with shafts attached and moulded capitals and a gallery above. There is great diversity in detail, a lot of interest and a lot to study. The long choir is lovely, pure Decorated in style (the sedilia of four canopied seats are somewhat restored) and behind the

altar there is a screen, really rather beautiful, of the same period. Selby Abbey has certainly had its share of vicissitudes and shows some of the scars; but it has great character and is well worth making that special stop.

Selby Abbey, crossing tower

❧ ST. MARY'S ABBEY

York   *OS 105 599523*

Ideally a whole week should be set aside to see York; the marvellous Minster itself could occupy several days, and there are many other delights both architectural and historic in the town. The abbey church of St. Mary is very much a case in point. The ruins lie just *extra muros* and across the River Ouse from the railway station, within the grounds of what is now the Yorkshire Museum. They are scanty but charming and what remains gives a good impression of just how glorious this church must have been.

It was a Benedictine abbey founded by William Rufus in 1088–9 but the building to be seen today dates from the second half of the thirteenth century. The wall of the north aisle is almost complete; it consists of eight large bays with lovely geometric Decorated windows which preserve nearly all their tracery (circles or foiled circles being the characteristic), and a wall arcade below. Part of the west front survives with its Norman window intact, and also the arch of the north aisle which leads into the now vanished transept. On the east side of this arch a part of the triforium can still be seen, again with geometrical tracery. There are the gatehouse, too, and a fair proportion of the precinct walls, perhaps more here than in any other English monastery. In the museum are preserved some large and impressive statues, and among them a specially important sculpture of about 1200 which may have been taken from the west door of the church.

St. Mary's Abbey is a glorious fragment; other ruins may have more to show, but few can rival its great beauty.

St. Mary's Abbey

61

❋ *WARKWORTH CASTLE*

Northumberland

arkworth Castle, on that magnificent stretch of Northumberland coast between Newcastle and the Scottish border at Berwick-upon-Tweed, has a superb site. It stands directly above the village, on a hill which rises above a loop of the Coquet, but a mile from its estuary. The river provides a natural barrier to the approach on three sides, although it is not near enough to serve as a moat, and on the south side, where there was no natural defence at all, a ditch had to be dug. Since 1332 Warkworth had been in the ownership of the Percy family, earls of Northumberland. The third Percy, lord of Warkworth, with his son, Harry Hotspur, put Henry IV on the throne of England in 1399; and much the most important remains date from around that period. The castle is now in the care of English Heritage.

The approach is undoubtedly best from the north; the mediaeval bridge is fortified with a tower, a rarity in England, and made necessary since the castle itself was never separated from the river by a curtain wall. The bridge is now somewhat marred by the erection next to it of a modern one (which could on reflection, admittedly, be a lot worse) but the view is unforgettable; bridge, tower, a good wide village street, and the castle itself piling up high beyond. It is thrilling.

The axis of the castle, like the village, runs north to south and entrance is from the south. It is quite a fortress, built of sizeable blocks of sandstone, pale fawn or dun coloured, squared and partly coursed, partly not. For masonry of the rough kind, it is excellent, and entirely in keeping with the character of the castle. There are a gatehouse, towers and a great hall, but the *pièce de résistance* is the keep or 'tower house' which you come to last, and this is how it should be.

The interest at Warkworth lies in its being at the same time the work of an architect as well as a military engineer. It is, as Nikolaus Pevsner has so perceptively described, the 'apogee of formal design and it proves the genius of its designer that it is at the same time a residence of considerable comfort'. The plan of the keep is a Greek cross, and within on three storeys the rooms are disposed most ingeniously; cellars, hall with minstrels' gallery, kitchen and accoutrements, a solar and a chapel which fills most neatly one of the projections of the Greek cross plan in such a way as the 'bevelled edges makes a perfect polygonal apse'! In the middle of the nineteenth century Salvin added to the convenience of the castle by restoring some rooms for the earl in fine high Victorian country house style, and to this day this is a Percy *pied-à-terre*.

A safe stronghold it always was, to which the outer defences bear witness; this was certainly a castle but one with real comfort within, a perfect blend of function and design.

Warkworth Castle:
the Keep

✣ ST. MARY, ASTBURY

Cheshire   *OS 118 846615*

The size and battlements of the church of St. Mary at Astbury on the eastern fringes of Cheshire appear fortress-like above a quiet village green; the lychgate plays the part of a barbican. The majority of the county's churches are built of the soft New Red sandstone – not always red it should be said – but unusually St. Mary is built of millstone grit, and this hard stone is the key to the church's splendour, for the details of the masonry remain crisp after five hundred years.

The church dates mainly from 1490; it was repaired in 1616–17 which gives the date too for the Jacobean furnishings within, and the spire was rebuilt by Gilbert Scott in 1838. The tower which is attached only to the north-west end of the church is rather plain and lacks decoration, especially pinnacles, but projecting beneath the parapets of the aisles there are some lively gargoyles. The nave walls are eight feet wider at the west end and converge noticeably towards the east, giving an effect of greater length, and this provides an interior of great excitement.

This wonderful interior displays a most stately Perpendicular, the King's College Chapel of parish churches! Seven continuous bays with no structural division between nave and chancel, and a fine lofty clerestory make for a feeling of spaciousness and light. All this is under a marvellous tie-beam roof, considerably enriched with

St. Mary, Astbury

bosses and a great pendant above the main screen. The south aisle has a glorious, still richer roof, with emblems of the Passion in shields and angels on the brackets; they date from the late fifteenth century and are in perfect condition.

The screen with its loft is on a large scale and of beautiful proportions. It looks about 1500 and less restored than most. It is a great ornament of intricate openwork tracery with some lovely carving of dragons in the spandrels of the central arch, and trails of birds and roses. A parclose screen (but no lofts) of comparable beauty encloses the north and south chapels. There are an exceptionally agreeable lectern, its wooden eagle complete with twig in beak, a splendid mechanical font cover, and box pews, all dating it would seem from the Jacobean restoration, wonderful enrichments for a church of real delight.

St. Mary, Astbury

THREE BRIDGES ACROSS THE RIVER URE

North Riding of Yorkshire　　　*Kilgram Grange, near Thornton Steward OS 99 192860*
Masham OS 99 226813
West Tanfield OS 99 269787

All these bridges are on the higher reaches of the River Ure as it winds its way down from its source in the Pennines above Hawes in Wensleydale. Below Ripon the Ure somewhat indeterminately becomes the Ouse and is then joined by the Nidd; thence it flows through York and, gathering in its course the streams of the Wharfe, goes on to Selby, Goole, the Humber and so to the North Sea beyond.

The bridge at Kilgram Grange, the most upstream of these three and to be found at the eastern end of the park adjacent to the Abbey of Jervaulx, is also the earliest. It dates from the fifteenth century. It has six arches (four main ones) and each shows prominent ribs underneath. It is both venerable and beautiful and has sturdily withstood the fast flowing Pennine streams which when swollen with the melting of the winter snows can become quite a torrent. Next comes the bridge at Masham, four miles to the south-east as the crow is supposed to fly, but half as much again by river. Its date is 1754. It has four arches, segmented again and with cutwaters, a good ashlar at the arch but a somewhat more rubbly stone laid in courses above. It is a lovely sight. Three and a half miles further to the south-east but almost double the distance by water, the river is crossed again at West Tanfield. Here the bridge, which has a probable date of 1734, is of three large arches rising at the

Kilgram Grange

centre, and the sandstone is a very pleasing blend of colours. The masonry is excellent and it composes with the castle, church and village beyond with the utmost felicity. Three beautiful bridges with no other crossings in between; a gentle morning's journey, and worth it for every moment.

Masham

West Tanfield

❦ *STONYHURST*

*I*ndustrial Lancashire tells a tale of machine-made brick and grime; but in the rural parts of the county much of the traditional building materials are still to be seen, timber and stone. There is stone in quantity; to the south it is a sandstone of a somewhat sombre pinkish hue, and the quarries at Woolton and Rainhill near Liverpool provided the stone for Giles Gilbert Scott's Anglican cathedral in that city. A carboniferous limestone makes its appearance along the valley of the Ribble, near Whalley and Clitheroe. Stonyhurst, the seat of the Shireburns from the late fourteenth until the eighteenth century, lies five miles north-west of Whalley, and limestone was an available and obvious choice when Sir Richard came to build his new mansion in 1592. Over three centuries a prodigious collection of buildings was assembled; in 1794 ownership passed to the English order of the Society of Jesus, and it has been ever since a boarding school for boys.

The approach is most memorable; a straight avenue, half a mile or more in length latterly between canals on either side, in the manner of Versailles, leads direct to a

Stonyhurst

68

gatehouse, an integral part of the west range of what might have been a great quadrangle. It was built in 1592–5. The gatehouse is a proud pile four storeys high with all the architectural orders, Roman Doric at the entrance arch, then Ionic, then two Corinthian, rising on top of one another to a battlement. Behind this just over a century later Sir Nicholas provided a flourish of English baroque – two octagonal turrets, each with a lantern open at the sides and a cupola in lead. It is a magnificent way to make an entrance, designed to impress, and impress it does, if in the course of its institutional life the windows have inevitably lost their original glazing.

In the gardens there are two identical pavilions, part of Sir Nicholas Shireburn's conceit and contemporary with the avenue outside. They may perhaps be just a curiosity, but each is a little gem. The masoncraft is very good; rusticated quoins, heavily moulded frames for the door and the two tall narrow windows, of six by two lights, that flank it; and above the door is a pleasing design of an urn with garlands, and a keystone which has the face of a Chinaman. The cornice is very bold, and the lead roof is swept up pagoda-style to its apex on which perches a large bird. The date is 1712.

The impact of Stonyhurst, visually, is its massive scale, and the memory of that wonderful avenue approach; once seen, never forgotten.

❧ WALLINGTON HALL

Opposite:
Wallington Hall

Wallington Hall, twelve miles west of Morpeth, is widely known as the house of the Trevelyan family generations of whom over a period of a hundred years or more made it a focal point for science and art, and filled it with collections of porcelain, furniture, pictures and many other *objets* of great charm. They were a brilliant family; Sir Walter and his wife Pauline the great patrons, Sir George Otto the celebrated historian, Sir Charles, eminent intellectual and President of the Board of Education in the first Labour government, and his younger brother George Macaulay, Regius Professor of History at Cambridge. They were fortunate to be brought up in such lovely surroundings; what a place this is!

The original house dates from 1688, the achievement of Sir Walter Blackett, and built on the profits of Northumberland enterprise – coal, lead and shipping, and no doubt helped by astute support of the Glorious Revolution that brought William III to the throne. The stone is a carboniferous sandstone, the material which figures most prominently in the buildings of the north-east. It is not the most beautiful of stones, and can be decidedly dour, but for strength and durability it is the best. At Wallington there was a quarry, now long worked out, in the nearby village of Cambo. Here the stone is an agreeable honey colour, partly grey, although the roof, likewise originally sandstone, later had the misfortune to be replaced with Scottish slate hauled from across the Cheviots. It is ruthlessly efficient no doubt, but also relentlessly regular, and too smooth a texture for the stonework of the house, but it is a pleasant grey and tones well. The Victorian chimney-pots are no asset.

Before the house passed through marriage to the first Trevelyan in 1777 it had been somewhat altered. The entrance was moved from south to east, the interior reordered, and the windows changed. Presumably none was sashed in the original house; now they all are but not *en suite*, nor, it appears, of the same date. On the entrance front all the upper floor windows have six by three lights, but below the three to the left of the front door are five by three, perfect in proportion and like those above but one pane shorter; then the five windows to the right revert to six by three but without thick glazing bars (which are the tell-tale of an early sashing) and are much too square by comparison. They must be later. To the south there are other oddities; the three at the centre on the ground floor have only one vertical bar instead of two, and the other six are all six by three, whereas they should properly be five by three. On the west, a subdued but very delightful front not really accessible to the public and glimpsed only through a gate, all look quite satisfactory and six by three on both floors. Lastly at the north, the service side and surprisingly dignified and unspoiled, all again appears as it should be. Quite a perambulation! Wallington among its many delights, is also for gazing at the glazing!

There are some fairly vigorous creepers, but apart from the *Clematis montana* to the left of the front door which is in danger of making too much growth, the

climbing plants – roses, honeysuckle, cotoneaster – are just right, reticent and not muzzling the architecture. Vigilance nevertheless must be the constant order of the day. To the north there is a stable yard – all beautifully put to lawn, and the splendid coach house with its clock turret is enormous. It dates from the 1750s.

The interior provides a lot of interest, colour and enjoyment. The entrance hall, dark grey and white is in good taste and two cupboards, one large with a red background, the other, smaller and much finer with black, provide a perfect show-case for a collection of some marvellous china. The dining room which has a screen of Corinthian columns has also been most successfully redecorated in blue-grey and white. It has a plaster ceiling, but no cove, of a fairly simple rococo design. This was the work of Italian *stuccatori*, the Francini brothers, and their showpiece is the saloon with elaborate plasterwork on a lofty coved ceiling to make room for which a bedroom above was sacrificed. A full-length portrait by Reynolds of Sir Walter Calverley Blackett, the owner responsible for the redecoration of the house and the introduction of the Italians in the 1740s, hangs in the place for which it was intended. The library, the dining room of the earlier house, completes the rococo set. The central hall, originally an open courtyard, was glazed in the middle of the nineteenth century on the advice of Ruskin, and given Italian arcades and a gallery. Dobson, the architect at Newcastle, was engaged and the eight large canvases are the work of William Bell Scott, an ardent follower of the pre-Raphaelite school. The paintings on the pillars are by Pauline, Lady Trevelyan, and a number of her friends including Ruskin. The hall is something of a Reform Club *in parvo*, convenient to the house no doubt, perhaps impressive, but not beautiful.

Another Lady Trevelyan, Mary,* wife to Sir Charles who gave Wallington to the National Trust in 1941, was highly skilled at needlework. She embroidered large panels to be seen in a parlour, hung with original Morris wallpaper of 1897 and furnished with a carpet from his factory which she bought at the closing-down sale in 1940. She did the needlework also on two very fine chairs which were made by her husband. Throughout the house there are some wonderful collections. Many great houses have displays of ceramics which follow the popular modish tastes of eighteenth- and nineteenth-century society for Oriental or French and German porcelain. Wallington reflects, in the many examples of English and Continental pottery and porcelain as well as Oriental wares of the highest quality, the more discerning judgement of its owners. There are also dolls' houses, regiments of lead model soldiers, and family toys, including a horse tricycle and a seventeenth-century dragon sleigh from Switzerland originally mounted on large runners and pulled by a horse. There is also Lady Wilson's Cabinet of Curiosities, a vast room of antiquities which includes a bust of Spencer Perceval, the Prime Minister assassinated in the House of Commons in 1812.

Some attractive gardens lie away from the house, across a road to the east and through woods. They are long and narrow running down a gentle valley laid out by Capability Brown in 1766. Below the lake there are flower gardens, the creation of Lady Mary. There is also a pleasant brick garden house and a terrace with many little lead statues of about 1700, which came from Holland. South-east of the house the public road crosses a steeply arched narrow bridge, the work of James Paine in 1755. It is most attractive with three arches, the middle one segmental, the other two – much smaller – semi-circular. The balustrade completes a very pretty picture.

Wallington is indeed a gracious house, full of interest and association, of different styles and taste. It still has the air of a famous family home, and it is paradise indeed for connoisseur and collector alike.

*On his visit on 8 August 1965, Lady Trevelyan, then 84 and blind in one eye, sought out Alec Clifton-Taylor for a few minutes conversation. Like her son, George, the artist-craftsman whom he would have known well as the Warden of Attingham Park Adult College where he was a frequent lecturer, he records her as having a beautiful speaking voice. 'To see George now, you wouldn't think, would you, that he was a shy little boy, very unsure of himself?'

❧ *PREBENDS' BRIDGE*

Durham   *OS 88 272418*

Durham is in a class of its own; there can be few more dramatic sites: a castle and a glorious Romanesque cathedral perched precipitously on a rock-girt peninsula dropping sheer into a wooded gorge below, and nearly surrounded by a great horseshoe bend of the River Wear. The rock on which it stands is joined to the 'mainland' by no less than four bridges, all now for use by pedestrians only. Three make steep descents; the Ewet to the east and the Framwellgate to the west, both originally built by Bishops in the twelfth century and both much reworked in the cause of widening and as a result of damage by flood. In 1962 came Kingsgate, at high level, spanning the gorge where the banks are most steep. It is designed by Ove Arup and made of concrete – and how much better visually it would have been as one leaping arch of shining steel from nearby Consett which was then in full production – and while it is renowned as a feat of engineering, it is not a work of art.

The best of all is the Prebends' Bridge (the term 'prebend' comes from the late Latin meaning a pittance or pension, and hence the portion of church revenues granted to a canon). In origin it dates from the seventeenth century but was replaced at the expense of the Dean and Chapter in 1772–8 after being swept away by floods. It was built by George Nicholson, Surveyor to the Cathedral, and his bridge, as to be expected is of the local Coal Measures sandstone, and consists of three fine arches with bold voussoirs and rustication at the bottom of the piers, and a delightful parapet subtly pierced at the summit of each arch. Unlike the other three it is on the level, and lacks the grace of those – such as Chester's Grosvenor bridge (p. 75) – which rise gently towards the centre. It is nonetheless a beautiful bridge in a beautiful wooded setting, rural to a point that it is scarcely imaginable that the middle of a busy town is but a few hundred yards away. What an escape! What a delightful riverside along which to stroll!

Overleaf:
Prebends' Bridge

❧ GROSVENOR BRIDGE

Chester

*C*hester was first prominent as Deva, an important garrison town of the Romans. It has come to be regarded, somewhat spuriously, as 'mediaeval', for in most appearances it is now really Victorian. The cathedral apart, most of the buildings are of slight architectural interest. There are two crossings of the River Dee; the old bridge dating from the fourteenth century, nothing special perhaps and with arches of various shapes and span, which detract somewhat from the unity all good bridges should have, and the Grosvenor Bridge, which is superb.

The architect is Thomas Harrison, who was highly regarded by his contemporaries,* and his bridge was not finished until 1833, four years after his death. It has a wonderful span, a single segmental arch two hundred feet in length high above the river, and at its time this was the largest stone arch yet known to be constructed. There are *tempietti* with niches at each end complete with pediments above. The stone is a mixture of Scottish granite and limestone from Anglesey and Westmorland, but is mostly a creamy-grey sandstone from the Peckforton Hills about twelve miles to the south-east. It is quite soft and easily ashlared when first taken from the quarry but hardens when exposed to the atmosphere. It weathers well and the bridge has withstood equally both the test of time and the pounding of the traffic.

Left:
Prebends'
Bridge

Below:
Grosvenor Bridge

The Grosvenor Bridge carried a new road which linked the centre of the city with the route to Wales, and in doing so drove diagonally through the old Roman street plan which had hitherto existed within the city walls. It was named after the earls of that creation over whose land the new route lay. Grosvenor Bridge has real personality; it speaks for itself and has form, dignity and repose. Of all the buildings in Chester it is the one which gives most unqualified pleasure.

*'Harrison has a spark divine' (C.R. Cockerell 1823). 'Almost, if not quite, the first architectural genius in the kingdom' (Canon Blomfield 1863). 'Only his isolation in Chester and a natural diffidence' writes H.M. Colvin in his indispensable *Biographical Dictionary of British Architects*, 'prevented his becoming a national figure like Soane or Smirke'.

SKIDBY WINDMILL

East Riding of Yorkshire   O S *107 021334*

Opposite:
Skidby Windmill

The windmill at Skidby stands on a hilltop just beside the main road halfway between Beverley and Kingston-upon-Hull. It makes, as nearly all windmills do, an extremely pretty picture. It is the only windmill left in working order in this part of Yorkshire, which nobody who loves England, least of all local people, can bear to call 'Humberside' the name of the new 'county' created by that insensitive and even insulting piece of local government legislation in 1974. Many people ignore the new address altogether; many long to see the name repealed.

The windmill dates from 1821. It is built of brick, the dark, brownish red often seen in this part of the Riding, but since being painted black it no longer blends as it did with another characteristic feature of the region – the pantiles on the roofs below. Skidby windmill is very elegant, tall and slight of girth, and must rise to a hundred feet or more, complete with its ogee dome-like cap of slatted wood and finial ball. It provides the focus of a delightful group, and is a striking and familiar landmark to the traveller along this road.

TURNER'S HOSPITAL, KIRKLEATHAM

North Riding of Yorkshire   O S *93 594215*

Only a quarter of a mile away from the ravages of the chemical industry at Wilton, near the estuary of the River Tees in the North Riding of Yorkshire (now lamentably restyled Cleveland), lies the eighteenth-century model village of Kirkleatham. It is the creation of the munificence of the Turner family who bought an estate in 1623 and whose patronage was to provide the village with four buildings of distinction; their own Hall, by Carr of York, demolished in 1955 and a dreadful loss; a Free School, a delightful and unusual composition in rose-pink brick and golden limestone; a church, and characteristically enough a somewhat

odd mausoleum by Gibbs just beside it, and a Hospital. This is a very handsome almshouse, founded in 1676 but rebuilt sixty-six years later on a most lavish scale.

It was Sir William Turner, twice Lord Mayor of London, who endowed the hospital for ten aged 'masters' and ten aged 'mistresses', and fifty-three was the 'aged' qualification. The buildings are large and dignified and ranged round three sides of a courtyard, enclosed by fine wrought-iron gates and a screen. This court-yard now consists mostly of lawn with a statue of Justice, made of lead, in the middle. The dwellings to the left and right of the entrance are low and two-storeyed, built of brick, reddish-brown with stone renderings, and roofs of Westmorland slate. There is no hall; at the main range the centrepiece, again of stone, is the chapel, with a lofty if somewhat ungainly steeple, flanked by two schools, each for ten boys and ten girls who would be educated up to the age of apprenticeship at fifteen. The chapel is on a generous scale, the size of a church indeed, and has a Gibbs and even a Wren-like feeling, though the architect is not known. It is lit by large windows, nicely glazed, and has fluted Ionic columns made of wood, and galleries (the one at the entrance stepped over the doorcase) to three sides. The best thing is the wrought-iron work, both of the communion rails and especially the balustrade for the balcony which is glorious.

For a long time Kirkleatham, being a charitable institution, and exposed at such proximity to some of the worst of present-day pollution, was badly in need of smartening up. Over the last twenty-five years much has been done through public and private effort to modernise the living accommodation and renew the fabric. It is vital, and now, thank heaven it seems certain, that this hospital and the rest of Sir William's wonderful legacy will survive.

Below and opposite: Turner's Hospital, Kirkleatham

RAILWAY STATION, YORK

East Riding of Yorkshire *OS 105 595516*

'This is York, this is York . . . York'; the announcer always seemed to be chosen for an authority of voice to match this magnificent station, for its train shed is one of the proud glories of the railway age. It is eight hundred feet long, two hundred and thirty-four feet wide, and one span measures eighty-one feet. It is supported on iron pillars crowned with capitals, and invites obvious comparison with ecclesiastical architecture, nave, aisles, even a blind arcade with port holes for clerestory above. It dates from 1877 and was designed by Thomas Prosser, the architect of the station, with Benjamin Burleigh and William Peachey. There are, of course, other fine train sheds throughout the country – St. Pancras, Newcastle, Bristol Temple Meads (where Brunel also had to accommodate a curve) and Paddington, to name but four. But York is the grandest.

Visually it gains enormously from being built on such a curve, for this gives a lovely perspective to the flow of the building, especially the vault. Doubtless sheds of these dimensions require enormous upkeep and lack not those who on economic grounds would champion their destruction. They should be resisted. Acoustics can certainly be a problem; announcements can be decidedly muffled even to the point of incomprehension, and no doubt the roof traps fumes from the diesel in the same way as it did from steam locomotives of the past. By the same token it must reduce noise to the city outside, and when properly maintained keep the weather out for passengers. York station conveys an overwhelming sense of stability and dignity – what more could an historic city ask of its railway station?

❧ EASTERN ENGLAND ❧

EASTERN ENGLAND

CAMBRIDGESHIRE ESSEX HUNTINGDONSHIRE LINCOLNSHIRE NORFOLK SOKE OF PETERBOROUGH SUFFOLK

Previous page: Harlaxton Manor

WALPOLE ST. PETER

Norfolk   OS 131 502169

What a church! Walpole St. Peter lies ten and a half miles west-south-west of King's Lynn in Norfolk, and stands in an open situation surrounded by beautifully kept grass, a large churchyard, and only two other houses, the former rectory which has the east end of the church for its garden (lucky owners!) and a pleasant old farm house. The church is a wonderful example of English Gothic: almost entirely a Perpendicular creation at its most stately, built about 1350–1400. Of the earlier church that stood on this site only the lower part of the tower survived a disastrous flood of 1337, and its rebuilding explains perhaps why, though dignified, it is comparatively plain and a little small and low for the rest of the church. If this is its weakest point, the exterior is in all other respects beyond praise, with its rows of clerestory windows, grand gargoyles, turrets and spirelets, monumental parapets, all extremely harmonious. The porch is very grand, two storeys with panelling and niches, two square bays and a good vault, carved at the bosses with some lively scenes, both religious (the Assumption and the Last Judgement) and secular (a muzzled bear and a dog gnawing bones).

The exterior is richly satisfying, but the interior is still better, quite superb; it feels almost like entering a cathedral! The nave is bathed in light; the huge windows are clear, and have lovely crown glass, over two hundred years old, and these together with the lofty aisles all contribute to the impression of airiness and space which are among this church's great characteristics. Even the modern stained glass in the chancel is fairly harmless. Everywhere the floors are paved with stone, and the walls show a wholly satisfying combination of light-grey Barnack freestone and colourwash to go with it. The tie-beam roof is good but nothing special.

The church extends to one hundred and sixty-one feet and at the east end of the long, aisleless chancel with the altar, it is raised ten steps above the nave, to accommodate and preserve a right of way – a vaulted passage, under the east bay of the chancel on the outside. If the raising was thus somewhat fortuitous, it was nevertheless a very lucky accident, for architecturally it makes for a fine point of climax, a wonderful piece of 'showmanship'.

The seating is mostly Jacobean and splendid in its general effect, but not particularly interesting; there is however a group of attractive older benches with poppy heads, and some with pierced backs, set to one side in the south aisle, and facing north, sentinel as it were throughout the ages; and in the chancel there are more stalls with lovely heraldic animals, and two of these stalls have preserved their old misericords, one with the pelican, which is an excellent piece of carving. The woodwork also includes some good fifteenth-century doors, an exquisite parclose screen of similar date across the south aisle, and stretching right across the church near its west end a Jacobean screen. This is somewhat ostentatious and not an enjoyable feature, and like the font cover of similar date with its octagonal spire, perhaps too large and elaborate for comfort. At the entrance to the chancel the

lower part of the original screen is preserved with its paintings of saints, a little crude and of historical rather than aesthetic merit.

The candelabra are first-rate and a striking addition to the furnishings. There is a huge two-tiered Dutch chandelier in the nave, very handsome and bought in 1701 for £33. This and the six smaller modern ones in the choir, of great charm, all hang from graceful wrought-iron suspension rods. A nice old poor box dated 1632, some good carved stone corbels to support the roof, and an early Tudor eagle lectern, very realistic, in brass and on an unusually slender stem, complete the picture. Even the 'ugly modern reredos' to which the Little Guide once referred is now tastefully concealed behind brocade.

There are doubtless many village churches with individual features to match Walpole St. Peter, but here it is the ensemble which offers such a wonderful and, once seen, unforgettable aesthetic experience. Patrington (in the East Riding of Yorkshire) notwithstanding, this is probably the finest village church in England.

Opposite and above: Walpole St. Peter

Cambridgeshire   OS 143 540802

The town of Ely, for it is hard to think of such an intimate little town huddling round its great church in terms of a city, is full of interest; the cathedral dominates every prospect for miles around, for at scarcely one hundred feet above sea level the surrounding countryside is among the flattest in England. In the Middle Ages, before the Fens were drained, this vast building must have looked like some great ship at anchor.

The most satisfying view of the cathedral is from the south, and it is here, beyond what was the cloister that much of the mediaeval precinct remains; a fourteenth-century barn, the Ely Porta (a great gatehouse dated 1397), the monk's kitchen and infirmary, and the jewel of them all, Prior Crauden's chapel. Crauden was Prior in 1322 when the collapse of the cathedral's central tower prompted the rebuilding of the octagon. The chapel indeed may have been completed earlier than the octagon, and stylistically there are strong connections with those who are documented with association in that glorious work, Alan of Walsingham, a goldsmith and a monk who became sacrist in 1321, and two Ely masons, Master John the Mason VII, perhaps on a consultative basis, his successor John Atte Grene, and William Hurley the carpenter.*

The chapel is built, as is most of the cathedral, of Barnack rag, a limestone from a famous quarry in the village of that name in what was the Soke of Peterborough. It is an upper room reached by a spiral staircase in its north-west corner. It has two bays, and the one to the west, lacking the tall Decorated windows, is almost by way of an ante-chapel. The nodding ogees of the canopies which surround the small windows recall the Lady chapel, and the niches above provide the parallel with the detailing of the octagon. The stone for the carving, as in the Lady Chapel, was much softer than the Barnack rag; it was probably a chalky material such as clunch, brought by water from Burwell which lies eight miles south of Ely and which lends itself more easily to the carver's skill. Over the centuries it crumbles and it is now in need of restoration. The authorities often now turn, wisely as they did in the Lady Chapel, to Clipsham, a tougher stone and one whose pale-cream or light-brown colour blends well with what was there before.

The treasure of this tiny chapel is the wonderful mosaic pavement, often hidden under carpets and benches and with its browns and yellows now faded over six centuries and more. It covers the whole floor, twenty-seven feet nine inches by thirteen feet seven inches in a most complex array of geometrical patterns; animals such as lions, stags and eagles, as well as vegetables and flowers. The centrepiece is the 'Temptation' panel – Adam and Eve with the serpent – which measures forty-four by thirty-two inches, a real virtuoso achievement: 'grand rather than pretty,' writes Jane A. Wight so perceptively in her excellent book** 'though the Eve has the wistful naiveté of some teenage idol.'

Prior Crauden's chapel is of course but a morsel after the feast, but to mix a metaphor it is of its kind a little gem, and for its historic and artistic connections, it is well worth a visit.

*Readers are referred to John Harvey's monumental work (with contributions by Arthur Oswald): *English Mediaeval Architects, a biographical dictionary down to 1550*; Alan Sutton, revised 1984.
**Mediaeval Floor Tiles*, John Baker, London, 1975.

❧ OXBURGH HALL GATEHOUSE, OXBOROUGH

Norfolk   OS 143 743013

It would be difficult to imagine anything much lovelier than the first sight of Oxburgh Hall. The approach through an admirable iron gateway, a descent through a fringe of fine trees, and there it is; a gatehouse of exquisite proportion, built of silvery-pink brick, seen between great beeches with glimpses of the moat gleaming in the sunlight beyond. In appearance, form, colour and texture this is superb, and quite incapable of improvement.

The house dates from 1482, and was built by Sir Edward Bedingfeld, whose family was in continuous ownership until the property was acquired in recent years by the National Trust. The north front of which this wonderful gatehouse is the centrepiece is the only part of the old house to survive, but what a survivor! It is a building of great distinction, intended as many gatehouses were to impress, and impress it certainly does; it is one of the most delightful examples of mediaeval romance and show. The colour and texture of the Early English brickwork is what makes this gatehouse so attractive; it is, on closer inspection, a beautiful dusky-pink, pink dusted with silver lichen, mellowed over the years with a delightful lack of uniformity, and the brick is fashioned to wonderful and even delicate effect. The spiral staircase, for example, in the north-west turret, has a hand-rail made wholly of moulded brick, and the vault is a piece of sheer virtuosity in 'plough-share' forms, remarkable for 1482 and only paralleled at Tattershall Castle in Lincolnshire.

The staircase provides access to some interesting rooms, hung with some rare tapestries, and (for those keen on historical associations) panels woven by Mary Queen of Scots and Bess of Hardwick. To step out on to the roof is another excitement, for here in close-up can be studied the trefoil brick corbels, made in two pieces for each trefoil and shaped in a mould. This is exquisite detail, and for such an early date, extraordinary. There are machicolations too, projecting parapets with holes in the floor through which could be dropped missiles or whatever onto unwanted intruders on the bridge below. On a clear day the octagon at Ely, eighteen miles away to the south-west, is clearly visible. The view to the east comprehends the whole of the gardens, a beautiful expanse of mown lawns on all sides, lovely trees to the north and a formal layout in the big lawn to the west.

Beyond is a walled garden, on the further side of which, at intervals, are four tall brick towers. They are Victorian but from a distance look surprisingly well – and picturesque.

Picturesque, too, is perhaps the most charitable description for the rest of the house, rebuilt in 1835. For the materials, it has to be said, by contrast, are rebarbatively uninviting, a poor brick dressed with a rather hot-looking terracotta, and the roofs mostly of dark, unyielding very mechanical-looking pantiles. How insensitive the Victorians were to materials! One bay window, to the west, can only be said to be in the tradition of the seaside boarding-house.

The gatehouse, however, is a real showpiece, and nothing can detract from its quality or its wonderful setting; this is perfection.

THE GUILDHALL, LAVENHAM

Suffolk   OS 155 916493

Of all the mediaeval wool towns in England, Lavenham is perhaps the best known and certainly among the most beautiful. It survives almost intact; a most impressive church, lavish with adornment, set on a hill and built mostly of stone, for stone it had to be for the most important building in the town. Below are the houses of the wool trade through the profits of which the church was endowed. For the merchants and the weavers wood and plaster had to suffice, and there is a fine array of half-timbering to be seen all over the town. Nearly everywhere the wood enjoys its natural colour and is never black. Over the centuries, naturally, much has had to be done to these houses, and very few look really genuine, but more recent restorations have shown a far greater degree of sensitivity, and they are delightfully pretty. The oak is mainly light-brown or silvery, and there is a lot of carving – some a good deal weathered – on corner posts, bressummers, doors and spandrels.

The Wool Hall is especially attractive, and among other enchanting houses the Swan Hotel holds high place. But the famous Guildhall of the Guild of Corpus Christi, which dates from the 1520s can once again rank among the best buildings in the town. The wood was always lovely, but now the cement infilling which once disfigured it, and even spread over the brick at the porch, has been properly replaced with lime plaster. It stands, like the Guildhall at Thaxted, on a brick plinth, and the modern bricks do look admittedly still a little commonplace. It is nevertheless a most handsome range, in a prominent position in the Market Place with good gables, an original oriel round the corner in Lady Street, and lovely hand made tiles. The carving on the bressummer which extends along the entire building at first-floor level and at the gables is very ornate, although it lacks the beauty of Paycocke's House at Great Coggeshall, sixteen miles or so to the south in Essex. The wooden figure, reputedly of the founder, the fifteenth Earl of Oxford, at the corner post is a delight. Within, the restoration is equally of the good taste and high order expected of the National Trust, and the Guildhall now provides an appropriate venue for a museum of exhibits of the mediaeval wool trade.

Because of the dearth of stone, Lavenham lacks something of impact, and is by no means the visual equal of say Chipping Campden, Burford or Stamford. But it has its own marvellously mediaeval spirit of place, and thoroughly merits its reputation as one of the showpieces of East Anglia.

❧ ST. MARY, KERSEY

For some the village of Kersey is the loveliest in Suffolk. It is beautifully sited, built not along but across the valley of a tributary of the River Brett about two and a half miles north-west of Hadleigh. The church has a spectacular setting high up on the southern side of the valley whence the village street spills precipitously down, across a water-splash – for the stream is shallow and there has never been a bridge – and then climbs steeply up the other side.

The church is well worth a visit; there is much here that is beautiful, and if it had not been for the senseless mutilations of the iconoclasts it would be in the first rank. It was completed in 1385. The flinty exterior is a little gaunt, and the tower which has a later date of 1481 lacks corner pinnacles and is a trifle stodgy. The flushwork of the south porch, however, is excellent, and it has a particularly splendid roof of a silvery brown oak with sixteen compartments all richly and differently carved. It was only uncovered in 1927. Inside there is a certain feeling of duality; the nave and the north aisle are about the same width and nearly the same height. The mutilations are terrible; perhaps the most striking victim is the historiated course of the north aisle which must have been both lovely and most unusual. The nave roof likewise must have been a joy, a combination of arch-bracing and hammer-beam construction, but all the angels are headless and wingless. What a mindless destruction! The

chancel was rebuilt in 1862. It preserves parts of its original roof, a plain arch-braced example of a simple type but with good cornices. There are other agreeable features: a fifteenth-century lectern, the stem of which is a gem of Gothic design, six painted screen-panels, all pretty village work, and a piscina, perhaps as early as the fourteenth century with a charmingly scalloped drain.

In the village there are many old houses, brick and half-timbered. One early Elizabethan brick porch is easily missed because it is smothered almost to vanishing point by a virulently thick creeper. Neither do the houses show much wood, for it has mostly been plastered over, and painted or washed in colourful array, not always with complete success. The apricot and lemon-yellow can look most attractive, but there are also a rather feeble boudoir-pink, and a bilious green and hideous magenta.* Colour applied to plaster can make for a pretty street but it needs to be in the best of good taste. Quite a lot of thatch survives, especially off the main street to the west, and many of these houses now look spruce indeed. Suffolk has always had more thatched buildings, including nearly twenty churches, than any other English county, and several hundred thatchers still find full-time work round the villages. Nowadays instead of the straw of wheat or rye, local to the district, it is nearly always reed (probably from Norfolk, but sometimes imported from Denmark and Holland) that is used. Reed travels well, however, and surely does not offend the *genius loci*. It is good to see the craft of thatching making something of a comeback and here at Kersey it is enjoying a delightful revival.

*There is a very persuasive section on 'Whitewash and Applied Colour to Plaster' in Alec Clifton-Taylor's *The Pattern of English Building (op.cit.)*, with a specially hilarious passage on the 'gastronomic galaxy of coloured succulence now available' (pp. 371–2). Readers are also referred to his excellent summary and discussion on the use of thatch (pp. 336–348). He came first to Kersey in 1936 in the company of H. Munro Cautley whose learned book *Suffolk Churches and their Treasures* (Batsford) was published two years later.

✺ THE GUILDHALL, THAXTED

Essex   OS 167 612309

The spire of the parish church of St. John the Baptist at Thaxted beckons for miles across the rolling and undulating countryside where Essex begins to look to East Anglia. It is one hundred and eighty-one feet high, and despite its somewhat weak little 'flying pinnacles' it is very fine and entirely appropriate for such a lovely church. Church and spire, set on a hill which adds greatly to their visual attraction and relationship with the town, dominate the scene, but below is one of the most familiar buildings in southern England, the Guildhall or Moothall. It is the subject of endless prints, engravings, watercolours and photographs, including the poster for the old LNER, and the dustcover for Pevsner's *Essex*.

The Guildhall, too, enjoys a splendid position, at the top of a wide main street

The Guildhall,
Thaxted

with a number of old attractive houses, and at a point where two narrow lanes fork to rise steeply on either side towards the church. It was built by the Guild of Cutlers in the fifteenth century. It is very pretty but does not by any means look now as it once did. It has undergone two major restorations, one in 1714 when the mediaeval gables were replaced by two hipped roofs, agreeably tiled – an unauthentic but not altogether unhappy juxtaposition with the mediaeval look below. Then in 1911, a much more drastic and brutal operation removed some of the earlier plaster-work, some of which was pargetted (decorative plaster-work which is very much a speciality of this region). Timbers were exposed, some still showing nasty marks where the pins which held the plaster-boards were driven through; other timbers were renewed and all were blacked. The original ground-floor arches were entirely replaced. In the much more sensitive restoration of 1975 no structural reconstruction was attempted, but at least the oak has been restored to a more natural colour, although a curious whitish wash is still in evidence. So the Guildhall is something of a 'deceiver'* but it is churlish not to enjoy it for what it is; a sturdy survivor, delightful in its setting and a much cherished focus for the daily life of the town.

The church, too, gives considerable pleasure. It is in the main built of flint, with stone for the spire and some of the dressings, and undoubtedly much in the overall appearance would have been gained if the material throughout had been of stone, but then there is not much stone to be had locally in this part of the country. There is much to enjoy; imposing porches with rooms over, a lively series of large gargoyles to say nothing of many smaller carvings, and a light and spacious interior, the best feature of which is a beautiful and grand example of a tie-beam roof over the nave. Relics of Conrad Noel, a famous vicar here 1910–42 abound everywhere. He was Chairman of the Church Socialist League, a passionate champion of social justice, patron of the arts and of the beauty of holiness. There are banners, ornaments, a painted lectern, rush-seated chairs instead of pews, and the occasional whiff of incense. Despite a certain arty-craftiness which still lingers on it would be difficult not to approve, for this is a church, like the little town below, which to an exceptional extent looks 'lived in'.

*and a 'gay' one at that, before that poor innocent word became hijacked, distorted and rendered inadmissible in any other than its present unfortunate sense – Editor.

✤ ALL SAINTS, CONINGTON

Huntingdonshire *OS 142 181858*

Opposite:
All Saints,
Connington

The church of All Saints, Conington stands almost midway between the parallels of the Great North Road and the old LNER's east coast line to Scotland, but is scarcely visible to travellers on either as they hurry on their way south to London or north to Peterborough and beyond. This village of Conington is now unfortunately, since local government reorganisation, declared to be in Cambridgeshire, and this is confusion confounded. For already in Cambridgeshire, but twelve miles to the south-east, there is another village of Conington. At

the parish church there, St. Mary, can be found one of only three signed monuments (and the only one that remains in this country) by Grinling Gibbons. It is in marble and a portrait bust of Robert Cotton, who died aged fourteen in 1697. He came from an ancient and influential family on whom Conington – the old English words mean the 'King's manor' – had been settled about 1460. Conington All Saints is also rich in splendid monuments, and the one to Sir John Cotton and his wife, who were Robert's parents and who died in 1702, has marked similarities to the signed monument, and must surely be by the same hand, although its authorship is undocumented.

The Cottons held the manor for about two hundred years and it is probable that the first of their line, Thomas, was mainly responsible for the building of this fine church. It lies in a park, close to the castle which was built by Cotton in the early seventeenth century and has since totally disappeared. The large church dating from about 1500 is all of a piece, and is an excellent example of the Perpendicular, especially the tower. This alone is built in an ashlared, oolitic limestone from the quarries of Ketton in Lincolnshire, while the rest of the church is rubble and cobble with dressings from Barnack as well as from Ketton. The tower is a landmark for miles around. The pinnacles, nicely decorated, were an addition in the reconstruction of 1638 and a decided embellishment, if perhaps a little too tall in proportion to the rest of the tower. Both the nave and the aisles have an embattled parapet, plain in comparison with some of the adornments of Somerset, but the windows, despite a certain irregularity, are very stately and give real pleasure and character to the building. An odd feature, and of some interest, is an octagonal stair turret in between the chapels and the aisles. This provided access for the sexton to the rood loft and the aisle roof above.

Within, the Victorians tinkered somewhat at the tower. They reduced the height of the arch by inserting a ringing gallery at first-floor level, and above it the mediaeval stone vault was replaced by one of plaster, not unsuccessful of its kind. Fortunately they left all the glass clear, with the exception of a very indifferent border at the east window which would be best removed. The arcade, surmounted by its clerestory is lofty and light. The piers are somewhat complicated; capitals only at the east and west, and at the north and south attached shafts rise from the floor to carry the main supports of the roof. In the chancel there are good sedilia, and oak screens, plain but pleasantly carved and both roughly contemporary with the building of the church, separate the north and south chapels from the aisles. The monuments are nearly all excellent. The earliest, about 1300, carved from Frosterly marble and full of feeling is the effigy of a young Franciscan vested in cowl with knotted cord at the waist. The rest, except two good ones to King David and Prince Henry of Scotland, erected about 1600 and carved in Ketton stone, are to the Cotton family; they make a memorable and rewarding sequence. In the 1970s the parishioners of Conington found the struggle of maintaining this large church beyond their means. It was eventually declared redundant, but has happily found a new guardian in the guise of the Redundant Churches Fund which set about repair and restoration with a will. It is a work well worthy of support.

ST. BOTOLPH, TRUNCH

Norfolk

OS 133 286348

There is a good deal to enjoy in the Church of St. Botolph, three miles north-east of North Walsham; some misericords, a screen of exquisite carving, as fine as any in Norfolk save Cawston, and a lovely single hammer-beam roof with horizontal angels of light-brown oak. But what, of course, this church is famous for is its font – or rather the elaborate canopy that covers it. This is only one of four in England. There is another, also in oak, in the same diocese at St. Peter Mancroft, Norwich, with which it has certain resemblances, although Trunch is smaller and later in date; there is also a seventeenth-century example at Durham Cathedral, and the earliest, the only one in stone, is at Luton, a typical product of the late Decorated style.

The canopy at Trunch dates from about 1500. It is an open octagon and the posts are carved with fascinating details and ornament – vines, thistles and lily being much in evidence. They support a fan-like vault, and above are eight sizeable canopies with overhang, pendants and ogee arches which might have been connected perhaps at one time to the posts below by flying buttresses and which thereby would have provided more stylistic unity. It has not alas escaped desecration by the Puritans; the carved figures which inhabited the canopies have now all gone and the painting is no more, but the topmost stage, culminating with a flourish in a large pumpkin-shaped finial is a wonderful show of Tudor opulence. The canopy at Trunch is perhaps primarily a curiosity rather than a thing of beauty, but it is memorable, has considerable personality, and is well worth that special journey.

Opposite:
St. Botolph, Trunch:
left – roof,
right – the font cover

❧ LAYER MARNEY TOWERS

Just as in the Middle Ages those who built and embellished churches and chapels vied with each other for grandeur and prestige, so did great land-owners with their gatehouses. Once considerations of defence no longer applied, pageantry and showmanship became the order of the day. Oxburgh, East Barsham, the Cambridge colleges of St. John's and Trinity, the royal palaces at Hampton Court and St. James' – they all had their gatehouses, but Layer Marney topped them all. It was built in about 1520 by Henry, first Lord Marney, Captain of the Bodyguard to Henry VIII, with a southern prospect over the Layerbrook and the flatlands stretching to the estuary of the River Blackwater and Mersea Island.

Fortunately to reach the church, which is pretty and well worth a visit for its excellent brick and tile, notable family tombs and some good woodwork, a track passes right in front of the Towers, with a fine view of the front, though not close enough to see the details. The house is well situated on top of a gentle hill. The huge skyscraper gatehouse dominates the scene, although a tall and none too shapely pine is competing for prominence all too successfully. The range to the east is modern, and that to the west much altered with additions in an ugly red brick. But the Tudor gatehouse is a joy; it has a lovely colour, rose-red with dark-blue vitrified diaper and chevron patterns.

The delight of this Tudor patterning – as opposed to that achieved by the Victorians with the relentless regularity of their machine-made bricks – lies in the variety of the headers both in colour and in tone, and also the extent to which they have been fired in the kiln. There is also at the windows and parapet a lot of ornament in terracotta; this is a fine clay mixed with sand and fired to make a harder, more compact substance than brick, which was then capable of being shaped and carved. It was an Italian fashion, introduced to England about 1510, and Italians were probably imported for the work here at Layer Marney. It is quite elaborate, though the colour varies; a biscuit colour (buff perhaps) at the windows, but for the shells and scallops on the top of the towers it looks whiter. It makes a pleasing foil to the brick; it can sometimes look, as was intended, a bit like stone, but of course it can be no substitute for the genuine article.

The present door, the main entrance, is not really satisfactory and it would be better if the archway were left open. It provides access to the north side, an elevation similar in design at the windows, but absolutely flat. There are no projecting towers, as on the south side, and it is decidedly much less attractive. This was to be one range of a courtyard to the north, never completed.

Layer Marney while it would not lay claim to being the most beautiful, is certainly the most striking gatehouse in the country.

CUSTOMS HOUSE AND DUKE'S HEAD HOTEL KING'S LYNN

Norfolk   *Customs House OS 132 616200*
                                             Duke's Head Hotel OS 132 616204

Three times King's Lynn was a strong East Anglian contender for inclusion in the BBC television series on English towns, and three times it never quite made it. This was mainly because over the last thirty years nearly one-third of all the buildings within the old mediaeval town have been subject to 'redevelopment' and in the process its soul has been destroyed. What is left is a collection of some good and highly enjoyable individual buildings – a number valiantly fought for and saved by a vigilant local Preservation Trust and some private owners. What the town sadly lacks, however, is cohesion.

Two buildings give especial pleasure; the Duke's Head, and the Customs House, the latter perhaps the loveliest building in the town and built in stone as an Exchange House in 1683. The architect of the Customs House was Henry Bell. He had been educated locally at the grammar school and later at Caius College, Cambridge, and had completed his education with the Grand Tour. He became a prosperous merchant, dealing in the production and export of linseed oil; he twice served his home town as Mayor, and turned his hand to architecture. His Customs House is a gem, neat, homely and compact. It has four bays below, an arcade formerly open to the street separated by Doric pilasters, while above, the windows have the Ionic

order in between. The top is not by Henry Bell. His design was a short steeple capped by a gilded figure of Fame and four obelisks. The lantern we see today, an octagon above pediments and arches dates from the mid-eighteenth century and surely is aesthetically an improvement. It needs only the arrival of a film company on location to provide the 'authentic, period touch'.

Henry Bell may also have designed the Duke's Head in Tuesday Market, now regrettably, for the other six days of the week, a vast car park and a very unedifying sight. He certainly was responsible for the Market Cross, an elaborate domed affair, put up between 1707–10 which stood in the market place until its demolition in 1831. The Duke's Head is a fine-looking house, nine bays wide and two and a half high, built between 1683–9 for Sir John Turner who had also provided the money for the Customs House. The house was to furnish accommodation for those coming from afar to visit his Exchange. Behind its rendering the Duke's Head still has some of its original brick, though some of the stucco above the windows looks early Victorian and the roof tiles now appear machine made. Nevertheless with its pilasters around the central window and its large broken semi-circular pediment at the centre surmounted by a smaller normal pediment above, it has decided personality and an imposing presence, undoubtedly the right address for the discerning traveller.

King's Lynn, because of the battering it has taken from the planners and developers, may reflect only a departed glory, but it is still a town with a definite style, and that character must in no way be allowed to be further eroded.

CLARE COLLEGE GATES

Cambridge   *OS 154 446584*

Where Oxford is industrial, Cambridge still has the feel of a county town. Cambridge has no street as noble as the High, but Oxford has no building as thrilling as King's College Chapel. Oxford was built of the local Headington stone which has weathered none too well; Barnack and Ketton limestone served Cambridge much better. Oxford has an unrivalled sequence of buildings around Radcliffe Square; All Souls', St. Mary the Virgin, the Camera, the Bodleian, the Divinity School, the Clarendon and the Sheldonian; but Cambridge has the Backs, and the succession of colleges juxtaposed along the Cam in a rural beauty Oxford cannot match. Oxford *in toto* perhaps has the greater architecture; Cambridge is decidedly the lovelier.

From the bridge at King's, looking north, there is a superb view, dominated by the glory of King's College Chapel, but in it the much smaller College of Clare plays a worthy part. It is built entirely of a yellowish stone, which could be perhaps from Ancaster, and belongs mainly to the seventeenth century. Though it was building from 1639 to 1715 and was interrupted for twenty-seven years by reason of the Civil War, it shows remarkable stylistic unity. The early work, at the east and south ranges of the main court was the work of John Westley, a master builder for whose buildings there is no documentary evidence that he was his own architect, but it is very likely that he was.

Clare has two gardens on the College side of the Cam and a lovely avenue of limes leads from the court to the bridge. Here Clare reveals its true delights. The bridge is ascribed to Thomas Grumbold. It dates from 1639–40 and has balusters set diagonally with stone balls beneath whose weight the bridge might seem now somewhat to suffer. It is a joy and composes very happily with the buildings both of Clare and its grander neighbour King's beyond. Best of all however are the gates, by Warren, 1713–15, excellent by even the very high standards of Cambridge ironwork; delicate and light, and absolutely *à point* in this delightful setting. His hand was also at work at the front of the college, where the gates are equally good with an excellent overthrow hung between some handsome piers with roses and festoons carved by Edward Pierce who worked at Sudbury Hall (p. 190). Clare College has much to offer, and there could be no better way to begin and end a visit than through these iron gates, as memorable as they are magnificent.

RENDLESHAM HALL LODGE

Suffolk   *OS 156 329529*

Rendlesham Hall, six miles north-east of Woodbridge, and all too close for comfort to the United States Air Force at Bentwaters, was demolished in 1871. But the two lodges to its park survive. These are follies, fantastic creations of the Gothick taste; one, Ivy Lodge, attached to a 'ruined' arch (looking about 1300) and rather amusing, and the other at the south-west corner of the park and far more interesting, Woodbridge, or Folly Lodge. To the eye both these lodges look about 1820, but the Department of the Environment prefers a date somewhat thirty years earlier.

Woodbridge Lodge has something of the appearance of a chapter house; it stands 'picturesquely' and somewhat surprisingly under six flying buttresses, three if you count a complete semi-spherical sweep as one. They cross, or meet, to support a central finial; it is all pure Gothick but, alas, rendered in cement. Each buttress carries a large pinnacle with niches below, mostly now the worse for wear. At first glance the central finial appears to lack a topknot, and why? It is a chimney! One only of the buttresses carries a flue, and has a trap door to help with sweeping out the soot.

The lodge is castellated and tiny. The main living area is hexagonal, but the rooms in the three arms of the building can hardly be more than eight feet square. It is a pity that the door is not original. It would be better with tracery and without a window (though perhaps this is an aesthetic rather than functional consideration), and white paint is not right; a colour to match the rendering is to be preferred. Rendlesham Hall Lodge would benefit enormously from some restoration and smartening up, for it is a splendid little building, as unusual as it is unexpected.

❧ KIMBOLTON CASTLE GATEHOUSE

Huntingdonshire

The castle at Kimbolton, which in 1974 found itself assigned to Cambridge-shire, was the home of the Montagu family and seat of the Earls and Dukes of Manchester for over three hundred years. It is now a school. Lucky people, for there is plenty to see and much to enjoy, let alone teach and learn! It occupies the site of a fortified manor house though nothing much of the mediaeval building remains. It is in all respects a late-Stuart house, an excellent if minor example of the work of Vanbrugh (architect of Blenheim and author of a number of Restoration plays) and his assistant Hawksmoor. There is some superb leadwork on the rainwater heads in the courtyard and on the south front, and within are some wonderful murals by the Venetian, Pellegrini. But the chief pleasure, and perhaps its greatest artistic attraction, is the gatehouse, the work of Robert Adam, built in about 1764.

The main front of the castle, with its great portico in the local Northamptonshire limestone, mostly from Weldon, faces east, and away from the town. Curiously enough (an anomaly explained by the licence classicists were able to take with mediaeval sites) it is not to this grand affair that the gatehouse is a prelude but to

the west front, the back as it were, for here was the obvious access to the town. The setting is a delight; the approach is from some pretty houses across a green, and Adam certainly did Vanbrugh and his castle proud. His gatehouse is an admirable precursor of what is to come; a most satisfying composition, strong and uncomplicated, with a hint of obeisance in its Doric elevation and balustrade to the portico beyond. The stone, it appears, is only a facing; brick shows through in the northern niche where the stone has cracked. The symmetry and counterpoint are charming: rectangular windows all correctly sashed within round arches, plain surfaces offset by rustication and Gibbs surrounds. It is all very harmonious. In order to blend with Vanbrugh, Adam restrained his more decorative style, and allowed himself only the lion masks above the gateway arch.

This then is not only good architecture, but a paradigm of architectural good manners, an example that will doubtless not be lost on Kimbolton school, staff and pupils alike. What a thrill to live on Castle Green and wake up each morning with all this as your front garden! No excuse surely to 'crawl unwillingly to school' at Kimbolton; but even if days spent here as a pupil, as indeed anywhere else are never, in truth, quite the happiest days of your life, there can be no other school that, architecturally speaking at least, can provide such a wonderful gateway to the wider world outside!

MARKET CROSS, SWAFFHAM

Norfolk

OS 144 819090

Most visitors to Swaffham, a spacious market town with some good Georgian and Regency houses, twenty miles or so to the south-east of King's Lynn, will make a beeline, and rightly so, for the noble church of St. Peter and St. Paul. This has a double hammer-beam roof of great beauty with a wealth of angel carving. First dally a little before the Market Cross, a delightful airy rotunda, classical and 'pure' and erected by the Earl of Oxford in 1783. It is made of stone with seven Tuscan columns supporting a lead-covered dome, and a figure of Ceres with a sheaf of corn on the top. It is very elegant, and a handsome embellishment to this pleasant and friendly little town.

❋ SAXTEAD GREEN WINDMILL

Suffolk   *OS 156 253645*

Saxtead Green Windmill, three miles north-east of Framlingham in Suffolk, is a pretty sight, its upper part weather-boarded and painted white above a three-storey round-house. It has four splendid sails – they are called 'patents' meaning 'open' – and are all in excellent repair. Behind is a fan tail, an ensemble reminiscent of some carefully designed mobile, as indeed it was. The earliest reference to date is 1706, and now this good and faithful servant is in retirement, though beautifully maintained in working order by English Heritage, and it may be visited in the summer months.

WANSFORD BRIDGE

The River Nene rises near Huntingdon, and wends but a short course of about twenty miles before it becomes canalised as part of the great drainage system of the Fenland that empties into the Wash. At Wansford, where there are lock gates and a quay, it was the boundary where for centuries a fine old bridge carried the Great North Road into Northamptonshire. Refreshment was available at the famous Haycock Inn nearby.

The bridge is a wonderful sight visible together with the inn from the not-so-new A1 to the left as one journeys north; and just before the bridge, about a mile to the south and not to be missed on the right, is the third of Wansford's notable

offerings, the railway station in the Jacobean style, now enjoying something of a revival as a place of pilgrimage for enthusiasts of steam. The key to all these buildings, and the hallmark of this region, is the lovely local limestone which gives the district so much of its character and identity. The bridge has ten arches complete with bold cutwaters. Starting at the north, the seven arches of the mediaeval bridge are dated 1577, followed by three, an extension contemporary with the building of the Haycock, of about 1672–4. Then comes the final and most recent leap to the south, a handsome, very wide, elliptical arch of 1795, ashlared and laid in courses and beautifully blocked and fashioned at the curve. It is the only arch nowadays that spans the water. A small round arch, a mere *soupçon* after all this, provides an afterthought. Very irregular it may be, but it makes for a splendid progress and it is well worth a detour away from the bustle of the busy main road.

❧ HARLAXTON MANOR

Lincolnshire   *O.S. 130 895323*

From the moment of driving through the entrance gates you will feel a sense of drama tingling through your veins. Ahead, a straight drive, seven-eighths of a mile long, dips and rises: first down and across a bridge, you see on your left an immense walled garden of Cyclopean dimensions (the walls mostly red brick, the only red brick here luckily); then, climbing now to a gatehouse, down and up again and here we are! An amazing ensemble of gates, screen, forecourt and façade. The whole approach seems contrived as a mounting crescendo of theatrical effect. What confronts us is a *feu d'artifice* of High Victorian fantasy. This is Harlaxton Manor, a great house, and one of the most extraordinary in England.

The design, dated 1831, is by Anthony Salvin, who was only thirty-two at the time, but a country-house architect of rising reputation. He was commissioned by a Mr. Gregory Gregory (sic), not, surprisingly, one of the new-rich for whom such flamboyance would have been in keeping, but a cultivated country gentleman with a collection of books, furniture, statuary, and other works of art. The building was completed and enlarged about 1838–55 by William Burn, a leading and indeed prolific Scottish architect. All the interiors and many of the Baroque features – and some are decidedly Vanbrughian – appear to be due to him, and his talented assistant, David Bryce.

The Gregory family lived at Harlaxton until about 1936. At that time, owned as it had been by a succession of bachelors and widowers, it was woefully run down, a mere shell with only one bathroom, no telephone, and no electricity. At the

eleventh hour it was saved from almost certain demolition by the eccentric and fantastic Mrs. Violet Van der Elst, a spiritualist, dedicated opponent and campaigner against field sports and capital punishment, and a musical lady who claimed the composition of over a hundred preludes, concerti and symphonies. She spent – and lost – over a quarter of a million pounds in refurbishing Harlaxton. This was a fortune made through the sale of beauty preparations and Shavex, the first brushless shaving-cream the manufacture of which she pioneered in her kitchen. When the war came and the First Airborne Division moved in – their Pegasus insignia is still to be seen in the north courtyard – she retired to four rooms upstairs. The door of one of these, her sitting-room, was said to be covered with a thickly-padded material which on being pressed exuded scent!

In 1948 the English province of the Society of Jesus bought the house, and the large estate that goes with it, for the reputedly paltry sum of £60,000. They too spent a lot of money on conversions, installing heating, a hot-water supply, a lift and large kitchens. It was intended that this should be a college for two hundred novices; there were never more than sixty. Within nine years the scheme was given up; a few Jesuit fathers came now and again for weekend shooting – and did themselves pretty well it was said. The house had become a tremendous white elephant. In 1966 the Jesuits granted a lease to the University of Stanford, California, and eventually, five years later, it became the home of the University of Evansville from the State of Indiana, under whose auspices it thrives today. Visitors are welcome but, understandably, only on written application; it is well worth the trouble.

The forecourt gates with their massive piers and porters' lodges are dated 1840, and therefore by Burn (since Salvin had been replaced two years before). They are on a huge scale, super-Baroque, monstrous, yet considerable imaginative feats and in some ways one of the most memorable features at Harlaxton. To the south (for this is a north-west front) is a gazebo, with an ogee cupola, very reminiscent of Montacute. The entrance front is undoubtedly the finest: Christopher Hussey (whose Country Life articles, 11 and 18 April 1957 are invaluable) describes it justly as 'Salvin's astonishing recreation of Elizabethan architecture at its grandest', and although, as he explains, there are obvious borrowings from other Elizabethan houses (e.g. Burghley, Rushton, Cobham, Northumberland House, Bramshill) 'there is little reproduction: nearly everything is redesigned and shows amazing assimilation on the architect's part (considering the date). . . .' After all, *mutatis mutandis*, this is exactly what Renaissance and neo-classical architects had done from the sixteenth to the early-nineteenth century. This front at Harlaxton is at least as good as any of the fronts at Burghley.

The south-east front (round the back, facing the hillside, for Harlaxton was literally dug out of a hill) is not symmetrical but full of originalities, especially the room with a stepped geometrical corner which projects with no less than ten sides, each successively changing direction. Despite the 'abstract symmetry' that for some makes this front Salvin's masterpiece, it is not as good as the entrance, and the elevation to the south-west is ordinary. This is further marred by the projection of an enormous conservatory (by Burn) which, however, has been most effectively restored through public and privately raised money, and not inconsiderably helped by the generous gift of one of his 'Dream House' paintings of Harlaxton by the artist John Piper. The stone throughout is a lovely Ancaster limestone, quarried only about eight miles away to the north-east of Grantham. It is light golden-yellow; in places perhaps too yellow. But the sunny hue of this stone is very welcome, and the masonry everywhere is quite first-class.

Within there are wonders to behold. The entrance hall is rather dark and strange, but the staircase to the left is well-lit and this makes for some quite dramatic effects. There is a white marble chimney-piece, *à la grecque*, which seems to have no connection at all with Harlaxton except that it is far bigger than usual. At the top of the staircase is a brilliant trophy of weapons, four feet across in wood, perhaps of cedar. The Hall, which the Jesuits had as their chapel, is on a huge scale, two storeys high. It has light-brown wood panelling, and a prodigious, if somewhat ponderous plaster roof, supported by hammer beams and muscular Atlantes almost driven to despair by the weight of their vast burden. There is a wonderful chandelier earmarked, it was said, for a palace in Madrid, but diverted here by the inspiration of Mrs. Van der Elst at the outbreak of the Spanish Civil War; and in the oriel, overlooking the garden, it is claimed, there is one of the world's largest pendants. The Dining Room is not nearly so successful. The ceiling is oppressive, partly because the room is rather low though here, as elsewhere, the university is engaged on a rolling programme of most colourful and highly appropriate redecoration. This room has

Harlaxton Manor: forecourt gates and screen

the central oriel – a very satisfying feature of the entrance front exterior – and through it there is a magnificent view down the drive and across the Vale of Belvoir to Bottesford church five miles away. The plate-glass is a real blemish.

Now for the most unlikely of staircases, and the most unbelievable, the Cedar Staircase. Are we in England, or that great baroque monastery in Austria, Melk? Or indeed in Italy? The lower part is poorly lit; the upper part brilliantly so. The well gets narrower as it goes up, and the sculpture ever more theatrical: here are shells, swags, tassels hanging on ropes, fruit clusters, huge scrolled brackets, again with toiling Atlantes, and aloft a winged figure of Time unfurls a plan of the house. There is a distinct feeling of France too – rococo, in the Gold Drawing-room with its two '*Galerie des Glaces*' effects, and again in the Long Gallery. This room runs the whole of the south-west front and is bathed in afternoon sunshine. It is the most enjoyable room in the house and has some first-class trophies and putti on the panelling. Everywhere there is colour; off-white, gold, dark-reds and blues, a wonderful display.

The skyline at Harlaxton with its towering central turret and its chimney-pots, spires and cupolas, is totally arresting and in effect not unlike Burghley, William Cecil's prodigious mansion just outside Stamford and that, said Defoe, 'looks more like a town than a house'. The scale and audacity of this building never cease to amaze. Yet somehow in their heart of hearts people may ask whether as a work of art it is really in the first class either outside or within and wonder what is wrong.

Christopher Hussey (*op. cit*) after fulsome praise of many things, refers to 'the essential vulgarity of the design as a whole because Elizabethan architecture is saved from inherent vulgarity only by genuine sensitiveness of handling or by its very imperfections either of execution or of subsequent decay.' Harlaxton, he says, 'has neither the sensitiveness nor the redeeming deficiencies of the real thing, but instead perfects the excesses of the Elizabethan age with the laborious but insensitive skill of its own.'

Perhaps; yet it is not the whole story, because the most exciting parts here are not Elizabethan but baroque. It is an unforgettable and amazing house, and for its baroquery, Harlaxton Manor is unique in England.

STOWMARKET STATION

Sussex   OS *155 052588*

Between 1847 and 1894 the Great Eastern Railway built a spur to their main line from London to the coast at Ipswich and pushed north to Bury St. Edmunds. For two of the intervening stations they turned to a local architect, Frederick J. Barnes, who built one of them at Needham Market in brick with some Caen stone, formerly closed but happily reopened in 1971, and the other at Stowmarket. Both stations are in the Elizabethan style. At Stowmarket, the station is all brick, a good red but admittedly looking a little too black for total pleasure, and offset by yellow here and there. It is a fairly sophisticated, symmetrical affair, with a rusticated effect at the quoins, recessed arches and some good-looking shaped gables. At either side there is a tower, polygonal below and octagonal at the first storey with a parapet above. It makes for a very pleasing group, well-mannered and right in scale and material for the town.

The railway age often made an important contribution to the architecture of England, and the successor authorities have not always been as sensitive as they should to their inheritance. Some of our most enjoyable Victorian buildings are (or sadly were) railway stations, and proper regard should be paid to their aesthetic merit. Where they no longer serve an economic purpose, suitable alternative uses (as at Richmond, Yorkshire, for example) should be found, and they should never be left empty, a prey to vandals and the weather. Happily Stowmarket faces no such prospect; long may it survive. To depart or alight at this station adds considerably to the pleasure of travel by train.

SOUTH-WEST ENGLAND

CORNWALL DEVON DORSET SOMERSET WILTSHIRE

Previous page: Stourhead: the Pantheon

✤ FORDE ABBEY

Dorset   *OS 193 359053*

As you approach from the east, across the River Axe (on its way to Axminster and into the sea near Seaton), Forde Abbey wears very much the aspect of what it always was – a Cistercian foundation dating from 1140. But go round the corner to the south, and there in front of a magnificent lawn set amongst ponds and yew is revealed a fine mansion. It is substantially a house of the sixteenth and seventeenth centuries, ingeniously incorporating a sizeable proportion of the monastic remains, and it now provides a comfortable and delightful home largely sustained, as it was in its mediaeval days, by the farming of a large estate.

The stone is a mixture of grey Dorset limestone, some large flints and as always with flint, a fair quantity of mortar. But in the main Forde Abbey is built of Ham Hill stone, as the stone from Hamdon Hill, quarried fifteen miles away across the border in Somerset, is always called. It is a limestone which has some oolite features (a shelly structure and calcium deposits) but geologists now refer to it as Upper Lias. It has a strong iron component, it does not endure particularly well, and is attractive to lichen. This gives it a somewhat spotted appearance which, far from being a disfigurement, can often be a positive visual asset. Unlike the more yellowy limestones of the Cotswolds it seems to absorb rather than reflect the sun, but nevertheless the subtle gradations of rich golden browns mottled with lichen on a sunny day give unending pleasure.

The main front faces across the cloister garden to where the abbey church once stood. It is a wonderful picture. It is largely the work of the last of the thirty-two Abbots, Thomas Chard, and Edward Prideaux, Attorney-General to Oliver Cromwell. Abbot Chard was building here between 1531 and 1543 as Leland recorded 'with incredible splendour and magnificence' and such extravagance to some puritanical tastes might well have been seen to be justification for the Dissolution. He provided his own sumptuous new lodging to the west (largely remodelled in the later building), a Great Hall, and the porch with its tower, all richly carved with lozenge and shield especially at the windows. He also reworked the cloister, again with a lovely frieze of stags' heads, shields and coats of arms of benefactors, and within the cloister is now a sort of conservatory, perhaps the most charming feature of the house. It is a gorgeous colour – all Ham Hill stone, and it has a very pleasing Gothick plaster vault dating from the early nineteenth century. The openings to the cloister are now glazed, most successfully, with rectangular leaded lights, and one section of the earlier cloister is revealed, built of a light Dorset oolite with Early English Purbeck marble shafts all on a much smaller scale but extremely pretty. Chard's Hall is unfortunately marred by later alterations; its west end is truncated, its north windows blocked, and while it has quite a good roof, the panelling of the eighteenth century at the walls is somewhat heavily and unpleasantly painted.

Prideaux, who was building almost exactly a hundred years after Abbot Chard, worked mainly on home comforts and the decoration of the interior. He introduced an imposing staircase made of dark-brown pine with big vases under the newels, which leads upward from behind the Hall to the Saloon. This has magnificently satisfying proportions, and the plasterwork is most impressive (as indeed it is also above the stairs). It has panels and oblongs with motifs of fruit, flowers, and other country delights. The walls were originally panelled and had pilasters throughout, but some of them now hide behind huge tapestries, woven at Mortlake and based on the original Raphael cartoons for his work at the Sistine chapel in Rome. The Oak Room (no oak to be seen!) again has an elaborate plaster ceiling, too low for the room perhaps and too heavy, but handsome enough in a strange if rather coarse way. Here the windows which overlook the garden, have diamond panes but are sashed, and have therefore rather an unusual zigzag pattern at the middle where the upper and lower windows meet.

Two of the former monastic apartments survive; the Refectory, now a Library, a little dark but with a good fifteenth-century roof exposed, and the Dorter (the dormitory) which in the nineteenth century was divided down its centre to make servants' bedrooms, seven in the range, and one at the end. From the outside the

Dorter looks truly mediaeval with its many little Early English windows upstairs, and beneath, in the undercroft with its rows of octagonal piers down the middle, there is a refreshment room.

The Chapel, originally the Chapter House, is Norman. It has two broad bays with much Norman work in the arches, and the ribs and the floors are all of the familiar Ham Hill stone. The mid-seventeenth century woodwork is again a little heavy and unhappily painted a dark brown, but relieved, fortunately, by some gilding. At the beginning of this century strange noises were heard from the undercroft. When it was opened it was found to be full of water and the coffins, floating about, were bumping into each other!

The Chapter House wing, the work of Prideaux, later received an attractive wooden lantern with a clock, both very likeable. There are stone slates now only on the projection to the west; all the rest appear to be Welsh. Although this south front displays the work of a number of hands, it enjoys a considerable unity. The crenellation helps; it is hardly a symmetry, although it hints at it in a beguiling sort of way. What makes the overall impression so memorable? The answer must surely be its lovely stone.

Forde Abbey

129

BARTON FARM TITHE BARN, BRADFORD-ON-AVON

Wiltshire   OS 173 824605

The church was the great landowner of the Middle Ages, and the Abbess of Shaftesbury ruled over the richest nunnery in the country. As an ecclesiastical landlady she was legally entitled to a one-tenth part of the produce of her tenants' farms and two enormous tithe barns belonging to the Abbey still survive. They were built to accommodate tithes, which were mostly the fleeces of sheep from the thriving trade in wool, and are far larger than many a church. One is at Place Farm, Tisbury, the larger of the two, although not the largest in England, with fourteen hundred and fifty square yards of thatching for its roof, and the other at Barton Farm, which is stone throughout. It dates from the fourteenth century.

The barn stands in a group with its farmhouse and granary just to the south of Bradford-on-Avon in Wiltshire, and it provides for the discriminating visitor to that town a far more rewarding experience than the much better known little Saxon church, which is surely of historic interest rather than aesthetic merit. Barton Farm Tithe Barn is a grand sight; the walls are of the local oolite, the same Bath stone as at Great Chalfield (p. 138). It is one hundred and sixty-eight feet long. It has as entrances, north and south, two 'streys', rather like the transepts, somewhat truncated, of a church. They are larger and more prominent to the north, the side which faces the town. The masonry of these streys is superb with big blocks of excellent ashlar, fine detailing at the sloping edges which shield the buttresses, and at the coping on the gables and the gables which surmount them.

The stone slates, or tiles as they are sometimes called, must number tens of thousands, and one day would repay a calculation. Roofing slates of this kind are to be seen everywhere in the locality and belong to a more fissile formation in the rock, that is one that splits more easily. This is known to geologists as Forest Marble and probably comes from Atworth, four miles to the north-east.

Wonderful as the sight of this roof is, the scale of the interior takes your breath away. It is tremendous; massive beams of oak with a span of thirty-three feet provide a roof arch-braced with three tiers of wind-braces along the whole length under the purlins: these are the horizontal beams which give longitudinal strength and structure below the ridge.

These tithe barns – and there is another in Berkshire (now redesignated a part of Oxfordshire) at Great Coxwell which inspired William Morris to describe it 'as noble as a cathedral' – are among the most magnificent secular monuments of the Middle Ages. The one at Barton Farm is rightly in the care of English Heritage. It is the most lovable of them all.

Above and overleaf: Barton Farm Tithe Barn

ALL SAINTS, MARTOCK

Somerset   *OS 193 462193*

Martock has the great good luck to lie only two miles from Hamdon Hill, and it is the same stone that provides, as it did for Forde Abbey and Montacute, the clue to the beauty of its parish church. How lovely it looks, a heavenly golden-brown! The tower perhaps may not be in the top league for Somerset; it is rather plain and could with advantage have been larger in proportion to the rest of the church, but at the nave there is a profusion of richly pierced parapets both to the south (the 'show' side) and the north although the parapet to the north aisle has to make do with plain masonry. The east end is Early English. It has five grouped and stepped lancets rising quite steeply to a central height, a manner more curious perhaps than beautiful, but it has decided charm. Sadly the lights are filled with rather indifferent glass.

The interior is indeed spacious, and the great feature is the splendid roof, massive in construction and rich in ornament. It dates from 1513 when the nave was heightened. There are pendants and a host of well-preserved angels who carry the king posts in the middle of the tie-beam. There is an abundance of panelling; Pevsner records that Kenneth Wickham, a perceptive writer about the churches of Somerset, worked out there were seven hundred and sixty-eight panels repeating six different patterns. In a fading light on first acquaintance you might consider the spandrels in the nave arcade to be rather like those at Sherborne, but on closer inspection they are more in the manner of Lavenham, the only example of the Suffolk motif in Somerset. The chancel arch is somewhat ugly and not at all a success, and the excessive width of the nave results in its loftiness not being properly appreciated. This is, nevertheless, an excellent church; there is much to enjoy, and the roof is among the finest in the county.

Opposite:
Barton Farm Tithe Barn

Overleaf:
All Saints, Martock

ST. GILES, LEIGH-ON-MENDIP

Somerset   *OS 183 693473*

Spires are comparatively rare in Somerset; towers are numerous. They are nearly all of the Perpendicular period. Generally they are lofty and beautifully crowned with pinnacles and embattled or pierced parapets and not infrequently they have niches with statuary. Many of the towers east of the Quantocks, and in the centre of the county, owe their quality to the beauty of the stone and their proximity to some of the famous quarries of the Great Oolite; those to the west are inferior partly at least because the stone is not so fine.

Leigh-on-Mendip (pronounced 'Lye') is six miles west-south-west of Frome. The tower of its parish church, St. Giles, is superb. It scores on all four points essential to a fine tower; the horizontal divisions are subordinate to the vertical, the angle buttresses have strength (visually and materially), the ornament becomes

Far left –
All Saints,
Martock:
left –
nave roof

richer as the eye moves upward and the horizontal divisions become loftier, and lastly the summit is at one with the sky, for if the tower comes to an abrupt conclusion, the eye will register an aesthetic jar.

There are three other important but not essential considerations on which marks can be assessed. First, the designer's handling of the stair turret. Here at Leigh it is within, but many Somerset towers, as at Martock, have large external turrets. In the finest towers this feature is wisely suppressed before reaching the summit, although the plainer can acquire an added dignity when the turret is carried above the parapet and surmounted by a spirelet. Then there is the arrangement of the windows, including those without glass which are really sound outlets for the belfry. Here at St. Giles they lack weather-mouldings, practically the tower's only fault. Lastly there is the relationship and proportion of the tower to the church, and while in the happiest of circumstances this will be a good arrangement, it is perfectly feasible and legitimate to consider a tower in isolation and on its own merits. At Leigh-on-Mendip, despite a most curious disparity in scale, the tower stands the test. It rises to ninety-one feet six inches at the top of its pinnacles (large, but not very large by Somerset standards) but the nave is only a third of that height, modest to say the least, and the chancel, quite insignificant almost, is half the height again. Yet this odd ensemble scarcely detracts at all from an admiration of this marvellous tower. It is a gem, the third finest in the county.*

Although tiny by comparison, the church too has its delights. It is built of a cool grey oolitic limestone, well covered with lichen. The stone came from a local quarry, it seems, and not, as might perhaps be assumed, from Doulting which is only about four miles to the south-west. There are a pretty little south door and rich pierced parapets on the south side of the nave, though not to the north which is away from the town. Within, the walls are a bit dingy and repointed with a dark mortar – a real pity. There are a tie-beam roof, with angels in attendance, restored but very comely, and some pleasing old benches in plenty, dated (by a former vicar) about 1390. And no Victorian glass! Hurrah!

* Alec Clifton-Taylor adored the Somerset towers; in 1946 he first made his list in 'order of beauty', and revised it twice, in 1958 and 1982. His top three never changed, Evercreech, Kingston St. Mary, and Leigh-on-Mendip. The others jostled for preference, but broadly speaking they settled as follows: North Petherton, Huish Episcopi, Ilminster, Wells St. Cuthbert (missed by many a visitor to the Cathedral), Chewton Mendip, Ile Abbots, Batcombe, Staple Fitzpaine, Mells, Taunton St. Mary and Bruton. After these 'top toppers' there came the 'good second class': Weston Zoyland, Bishop's Lydeard, Hinton St. George, Weare. Others for consideration, *proxime accessit* in no particular order, are listed as: Wellington (Devon type), Glastonbury St. John, Taunton St. James, Ruishton, Chew Magna, Kilmersdon, Winscombe, Lympsham, Portishead and Norton-sub-Hamdon. For a fuller discussion of his views on Somerset Towers, his *English Parish Churches as Works of Art* (Batsford, 1974) in particular pp. 96–99, makes fascinating and highly entertaining reading. He also recommends three other sources: F. J. Allen, *Great Church*

Towers of England (1932), A.K. Wickham, *Churches of Somerset* (1952) and the reclassification in Nikolaus Pevsner's two Somerset volumes in *The Buildings of England* (1958). 'Allen is the fullest,' he writes, 'Pevsner and Wickham the soundest.'

St. Giles,
Leigh-on-Mendip

GREAT CHALFIELD MANOR

The chalk downs of Wiltshire were excellent for pasture; 'they are all hilly' wrote Daniel Defoe in 1724, '. . . plains and grassy downs for breeding and feeding vast flocks of sheep.' The mediaeval wool trade brought much prosperity to the area, and on its profits, Thomas Tropenell, a rich clothier, Member of Parliament and of Lincoln's Inn built himself his manor house at Great Chalfield, three miles north-east of Bradford-on-Avon which in the Middle Ages was one of the most flourishing wool towns in the county.

The house dates from about 1470; its setting is exquisite. The approach is across water, not a moat, but part of a leat, made by damming a stream half a mile away to provide water to power a mill-wheel which still survives. Water therefore surrounds the house, at a lower level to the rear, but on the entrance side, the north, it makes a most romantic sight, full of reed and bullrush, a haven for the spotted flycatcher. To the west is a substantial range with a good-looking barn, and to the east is the small but beautifully kept and furnished church of All Saints, nominally the parish church but in effect the chapel of the estate. The group is most memorable.

This is limestone country, and everything here is built of the local stone, from Hazelbury above Box, one of a group known generically as Bath stone. The walls are of rubble, the dressings of superb ashlar. The roof is of stone slates and as with all stone roofs before the nineteenth century, the slates are carefully graded and laid in courses of gradually diminishing size, from the broadest at the eaves to the narrowest at the ridge. The house has an intriguing but imprecise symmetry. At the centre is the great hall which rises through the whole height of the building, and it is flanked by dining-room, solar, family and guest bedrooms, all under fine gables to which some excellently carved finials – dog, griffon, knight and the like – provide a fitting flourish. The oriel windows to east and west are very handsome and a memorable feature of this façade.

On the whole the house is decidedly less good within than without. The hall is well lit, and has an almost flat roof, but the paint is now somewhat faded and the bosses horribly mutilated, in fact cut in half. The massive beams are said to be original and there are scrolls bearing Tropenell's motto – *'le joug tyra belement'*, 'the yoke drew well', or more loosely translated 'Farming pays'! There is a gallery at the west end, and three masks, carved in stone with large eyes, serve as caches from which could be observed the goings on in the hall below.

The dining-room is dark. It has a plaster ceiling, added along with the oak panelling (which now looks almost all renewed) about seventy years after the house was built. Upstairs the smaller oriel to the west lights the north bedroom which has a timber arch-braced and collar-beam roof open to the ridge. It is a good domestic example and provided the model for a renewal of the roof in the solar in 1913. Here the roof is lit by the more elaborate oriel, and this has on its inside a delightful little pendant vault.

At the rear of the house, a wing projects to the south-west, a half-timbered and quite good restoration of 1910, but despite the re-use of ancient timbers, it looks somewhat out of place. Nonetheless it makes for a much larger house than would first appear from the other side. The manor house is set in an old English garden that complements it to perfection, with the added bonus of the most unusual and beautifully kept *tempietti* in yew, each with four 'gables'. Five hundred years ago, remote as it was, and still is, in the country, Great Chalfield had to be self-supporting with its own farm, dairy, brewhouse, mill and even fish stews the remains of which are still to be seen on the lower stretch of water to the south of the house. It is a precious survivor, an evocation of life lived on the mediaeval manor, a reminder of an age of sturdy self-reliance.

139

THE GEORGE INN, NORTON ST. PHILIP

Somerset

The village of Norton St. Philip is perched on a ridge at a crossing of two routes and the George Inn, one of the most memorable inns in the country, stands at the crossroads, most convenient for attracting the thirsty traveller from all directions. It has been here for at least five hundred years or longer first as a grange and then as a guest house of the Carthusian monastery at Hinton Priory.

Unusually for this area, where nearly everything substantial is built of the local limestone, the top two storeys on the side facing the road show timber and plaster, although the roof has stone slates. At the first floor there are three delightful oriel windows, irregularly placed in relation to the rest of the fenestration, and a handsome stone arch which leads to a courtyard beyond. This front is sturdy, robust and full of character. From the courtyard, paved with stone slabs, the back of the house all appears to be stone, with a projecting stair-turret, some mediaeval-looking two-light windows, stone roofs, a few more recent pantiles, and a gallery again showing wood and plaster. The stone is nearly all rubble and most appropriate.

Within, what little restoration and rearrangement has been required over the years has been achieved, mercifully, with the utmost discretion. The George, thankfully, is in excellent hands. It is among the finest and most venerable of England's hostelries, but vigilance is constantly needed lest anything should ever be allowed to spoil the atmosphere of this most mediaeval of inns.

ST. ANDREW, CULLOMPTON

*Below and overleaf:
St. Andrew,
Cullompton*

Devon is England's sandstone county *par excellence*, and after the cathedral at Exeter, the church dedicated to St. Andrew at Cullompton is undoubtedly its finest. This is a beautiful church, a most noble example of late Perpendicular, and takes a full hour to see properly. The first impression of the exterior is one of delightful soft colours: an amethystic, pale purply-red sandstone, the local one, offset with grey-white dressings of Beer stone. This is a limestone, the nearest available, but it is too soft to withstand the climate and decays badly, so it is in need of constant patching.

The tower, Devon-type and the last part of the church to be built, dates from the decade of the Reformation 1545–9. It is over one hundred feet high, lovely in its proportions and rich in ornament. It has pretty pierced tracery to its two-light belfry windows, buttresses alive with gargoyles, and its top is crowned with battlements, pinnacles, crockets, and no less than three weather-vanes: what a sumptuous array for a parish church! But the showpiece both without (and within as we shall see) is the famous Lane Aisle, built by John Lane, a wool merchant, and added to the south of the church's nave in 1525–6.

Why should he build on this scale, enlarging a church already more than big enough for the town? The reason is to be seen in the nearby town of Tiverton a few miles away, where John Greenaway, an equally prosperous merchant, had added a porch and chapel to the parish church in a stylish display of ostentation, fully adorned with carvings of ships, and a personal monogram many times repeated drawing attention to his munificence.

So across the hill at Cullompton, not to be outshone, John Lane built not just a chapel but a whole aisle, enriched too with plenty of carving – sheep-shearers, shipping, the astrological symbol for tin, and of course monograms. It makes for a resplendent skyline, in the exact sense of the word; it is a spectacular achievement.

Within the church, John Lane, in a gesture of splendid opulence, adorned his aisle with a fan vault; it is perfectly preserved. The tracery is of masterly assurance and the pendants have emblems of the Passion and, again, sheep-shearers and the symbol for tin. The vault closely recalls the retrochoir at Peterborough – stylistically almost without doubt the work of John Wastell, who was responsible for the vaulting in King's College Chapel, Cambridge. Nevertheless, Nikolaus Pevsner is probably correct in tracing the derivation from Sherborne, about 1475, via the Dorset Aisle at Ottery St. Mary.

This is a grand interior, six bays of nave with aisles and the Lane Aisle in addition, so it is large and long, and light floods in through lofty Perpendicular windows. There is no chancel arch and architecturally the nave and the choir are continuous. The special beauty is the roof, lit over the nave, unusually for Devon, by a clerestory. This is a cradle roof, finely coloured, but, though continuous, there is a change of

Right and far right:
St. Andrew,
Cullompton

colour over the choir, crimson and gold on a ground of *terre verte*, while over the nave the scheme is Indian red and pale brown on a pale light-blue ground. There is an abundance of angels and arabesques, quite a *corps de ballet*! The north and south aisles have pleasant grey and red flat panelled roofs. The rood beam, in effect a tie-beam with a small royal arms over the centre, is unusual and rather unliturgical!

There is more to see yet; the rood screen stretches across chancel and both aisles. It looks splendid, with three trails and double cresting, decorated with a twisting 'Maypole' motif but unluckily the colouring is overdone. Then there is a Jacobean gallery supported on squat Ionic pillars. The walls are not white, but cream-coloured but it would be the better if the oak pews were drastically reduced in number. But to cavil risks being pernickety: in so many ways this is a glorious church.

The Lane Aisle:
St. Andrew,
Cullompton

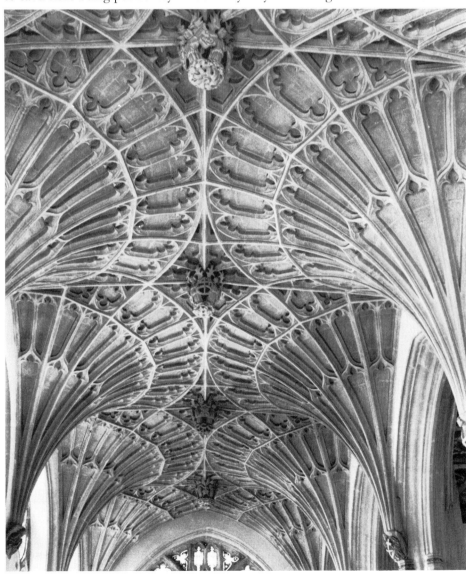

MARKET CROSS, MALMESBURY

Until 1962, the best way to approach Malmesbury would undoubtedly have been by train, locally and somewhat quaintly known as the Bunk, a push-me-pull-you two-coach affair, up a branch line west of Swindon on Brunel's famous London to Bristol Great Western. Now the more likely approach is from the south by Exit 17 on the M4, or through Stroud and Cirencester from the north.

Whichever way you come, Malmesbury announces itself from quite a way off, for this is a hill-top town, fortified since the days of Alfred, surrounded on three sides by the Bristol Avon, and dominated by its Benedictine abbey church, a mutilated but magnificent fragment of its former glory. It is still the parish church, renowned for the prodigious if somewhat fanciful romanesque carving of its south porch, now beautifully restored and cleaned.

Wiltshire is a chalk county, full of downs and grazing sheep, and Malmesbury was a thriving wool town well into the eighteenth century. Here in the north, the county boundary almost hugs the line of the Great Oolite, so Malmesbury is decidedly a stone town, looking more to the Cotswolds than to the chalk, and its proximity to some of the most famous quarries of the oolite must explain the appearance of its abbey, and also its Market Cross.

The Cross, built about 1500, stands just outside the Abbey precincts to the south, and is best seen from the High Street which curls its way up from the bridge over the Avon below. It marks too the junction of routes within the town to Bristol and Oxford, and despite a bypass to the east, it still is occasionally involved in a brush with all too large lorries having to negotiate narrow streets. The stone is ashlar, a somewhat dour non-reflecting shade of grey. On closer inspection it reveals quite a lot of white, tempered no doubt by three restorations over the last two hundred years, the most recent (a somewhat patchy affair) in 1980 for the borough's eleven hundredth anniversary celebrations. For this the stone came from Monk's Park near Corsham. In its various restorations, the Cross has happily escaped the hands of the 'improvers', and it looks today much as it must have done when John Leland the Tudor historian saw it in 1542 and wrote: 'It's a right faire costley peace of worke, made all of stone, curiously vaulted for poore market folkes to stand dry when rayne cummith.' There is no longer a market at the Cross, but it still serves occasionally as a useful venue for vendors of home-made produce, and a convenient and perhaps even romantic rendezvous for residents.

The Cross is certainly one of the best in England. It is octagonal, forty-one feet high with four-centred arches on all its eight sides. In three spandrels on the west are carvings of leaves, grapes, acorns and vines. This vault is lierne (from the French 'lier' – to tie) and springs from a central shaft which at its base provides a useful undercover sitting area. Above the arches is a battlement and the buttresses of the main structure end in jolly crocketed pinnacles and gargoyles. From the battlement spring flying buttresses in jaunty curves; they carry a kind of lantern

which in turn is octagonal, and culminates in a spirelet which again echoes the pinnacles below. It has niches with statues of saints and a delicately carved Crucifixion.

Opposite:
Market Cross,
Malmesbury

Malmesbury's Market Cross invites obvious comparison with two contemporaries; at Salisbury where the Poultry Cross (a mere hexagon) is the only one of that city's four mediaeval crosses to survive, and the Market Cross at Chichester built of Caen stone, a present from its bishop and like Malmesbury's, octagonal. Both Salisbury and Chichester have been marred by later accretions; Salisbury had the bad luck to have a new top in 1853, and Chichester, more happily but still inappropriately received a cupola in 1743. Malmesbury is altogether a more artistic unity.

It is a pity the Malmesbury Cross has to be disfigured by roadsigns, admittedly at pavement level, and sometimes by vehicles parked behind it, and at festive times, bunting and fairy lights on the houses beyond. For this Cross deserves the very best; it is a great visual asset to the town, a surprise and delight to visitors, a justifiable source of borough pride.

❁ BARRINGTON COURT

Somerset   OS 193 397183

Barrington Court is to be found at the end of a village of that name, four miles north-east of Ilminster, and the walk from the lane to the house is idyllic, through orchards of apples and pears with the promise of a walled garden to see later. Nothing, however, is so beautiful as the south garden front, previously the entrance and now so again. It is not quite symmetrical, but almost, beguilingly so, and a long hard look is needed to detect that to the right of the porch there are two rather than one four-light windows, and a small bay, formerly the staircase, both arrangements for the Hall. The huge lawn is a perfect foil for the golden Ham Hill stone which is such an enormous asset to the whole of this district. Even the rather blotchy appearance occasioned by lichen to which it is always a prey is extremely attractive; it adds venerability to a building already dignified with age.

The house has long been credited to Henry Daubeney and dated 1514, but there is apparently no documentary evidence for this, and the E-plan lends itself more to the mid-sixteenth century, the creation perhaps of William Crofton, a rich Norfolk merchant who lived here from 1559 until 1564. The windows are all transomed, mullioned and hood-moulded and have leaded lights, though not of diamond pattern, and the eye is led easily upward to a fine array of chimneys and finials on the gables, all spiral in stone and 'set along the skyline like giant chessmen'.* Colonel A. A. Lyle took a lease on the property in 1920 (seven years after it had passed to the National Trust, its present owners) and he did great service in stripping off the slates and putting back a stone roof. He found what was virtually a derelict farmhouse, and now it is altogether a splendid survivor for which we should be eternally grateful, but on balance it might have been better if he had not been quite so drastic or quite so lavish. For Barrington Court, the house and even the grounds were refurbished in millionaire style, and the interior, for all its splendour *is* rather reminiscent of Liberty's! A great deal – for example the whole of the magnificent staircase – looks suspiciously like reproduction stuff and Colonel Lyle had a real craze for oak panelling which is all over the house, linenfold, genuine no doubt, but from elsewhere; then there are a timber roof from Hereford, and an early sixteenth-century screen from King's Lynn. Colonel Lyle filled the house with beautiful and expensive furniture, not particularly *au courant*, which while it may have nourished the body did little for its soul. Recently a new lessee has arrived, and the furniture has been dispersed.

To the west lies the stable quadrangle, which is quite different and built in about 1670 by the Strode family who lived here for one hundred and fifty years. It is brick with yellow stone dressings. The building has seen two restorations, the most recent in the 1920s. It has thereby lost much of its character particularly to the west where the delightful walled garden is situated. Plans for the planting were submitted for suggestions and approval to none other than Gertrude Jekyll, Lutyens' collaborator, and doyenne of English country garden designers. Some of her suggestions may have been followed but this is a garden which is predominantly modern in feeling.

Barrington Court is lovely, with the south front as its outstanding feature, and since its restoration is undoubtedly one of the finest buildings of its date in England.

The National Trust Guide, compiled and edited by Robin Fedden and Rosemary Joekes, Jonathan Cape, rev. 1977.

Barrington Court

❦ MANOR HOUSE, SANDFORD ORCAS

The Manor House at Sandford Orcas, three miles north-north-west of Sherborne, a perfect example of its type and period, dates from about 1533, and it is substantially unaltered. The approach is through a gatehouse with a bedroom above to the north side of the house, which makes for quite a distinguished feature of the setting. The entrance front faces east, and rather surprisingly turns away from the road. It is decidedly irregular, and even more so before the gable to the north was built up (and not without sensitivity for the rest of the building) in the late nineteenth century. The stone is at first deceptive; it is a greyish colour – not a pure grey, but there is little gold in it and only touches here and there of a pale yellow-brown; yet the consensus is now that it is from Hamdon Hill. It lends itself, needless to say, to some admirable detailing, especially at the porch with its octagonal buttresses, the coat of arms, and lions carved on the shields of the finials. The roofs too, very properly, are all of stone.

The windows at the south-east corner (at either side) are superb; each is of two bays, with the windows at ground floor twice the height of those at the first storey, a feature which gives both character and identity to the house. They tell a tale, too, for here the mediaeval arrangement of hall and solar has been set aside, and the hall is but the ground floor only with a chamber above.

This was never a grand house nor a particularly convenient one to live in, for compared with later country houses, it lacks space, some of the rooms are a little dark, and there are lots of stairs, including two spiral staircases. Four-poster beds here would surely have to have been erected in the rooms *in situ, in toto*! All in all this is a house full of atmosphere and the flavour of its time, engaging and arresting in its interest.

❧ BINGHAM'S MELCOMBE

Dorset   OS 194 773022

Bingham's Melcombe lies half a mile across fields from Melcombe Bingham in a remote part of Dorset, one of England's most beautiful and unchanging counties, about ten miles south-west of Blandford Forum. The parish church of St. Andrew stands in the grounds of the house, yet the parish of Melcombe Horsey takes its name from Higher Melcombe, two miles to the west where another mediaeval manor was built for a Sir John Horsey.

The house, in the ownership of the Bingham family for over six hundred years until 1895, is built round three sides of a courtyard. Broadly speaking it is of three dates and is on two levels. The earliest part is the gatehouse, nothing special, which guards the approach from the south. It was once freestanding, and some have dated its origin as early as the fourteenth century, but it was later extended with quite a spacious range and joined the west wing (kitchen and services) in the seventeenth century. Substantially the rest of the house is Tudor, although there are some eighteenth-century additions at the north-east and at the dining-room round to the north-west; the interior of the hall is Victorian. Rather unexpectedly the house is not entirely of limestone. There are also considerable quantities of flint (Dorset being on the chalk). It appears in bands, only at intervals, used as it were to eke out the silver-grey Ham Hill ashlar. At the north-west in a gable there is a chequer pattern, not unlike the flush-work of some of the Suffolk churches. The flints admittedly are squared and knapped, and provide an agreeable decorative foil. The roofs are all of stone. There is a somewhat small and cramped courtyard; the west range is low and quite inoffensive but of no special interest and the gatehouse, despite its one early-seventeenth century panelled room upstairs, is externally fairly poor. Moreover, placed as it is at the south, it hides the sun, and obscures the view.

The most exciting external feature of the house is the oriel – the great two-tier bay of the hall and room above. Between the two storeys is the Bingham coat of arms, rich and deeply cut, with scrolls, foliage and acanthus leaves, and shafts

to either side which soar up to end in finials above the roof. This in turn is echoed by the octagonal shafts at the corner of the bay which also have finials at the gable, and this linear vertical arrangement provides a cohesive and most satisfying composition. The oriel is much in the style of the one which was at Clifton Maybank before its demolition and it is more than an informed guess that Sir John Horsey of Higher Melcombe, who also owed Clifton Maybank fifteen miles to the north-west near the Somerset border; may have made a friendly recommendation. The coat of arms too has distinct affinities with Clifton Maybank, and this it *is* possible to compare, for it turns up reset as the frontispiece on the north entrance at Montacute (p. 156). The large houses of Dorset were obviously quite keen on this traffic for in 1966 the entrance porch from Tyneham (where the house was being taken down and reconstructed at Athelhampton) was reset here at Bingham's Melcombe. It is one-storey and in the move has lost a gable, but the date, 1583, is about right, and it now serves a useful purpose and clearly has found a good home.

There is much to see inside. The hall, despite its Victorian reworking, has kept many of its original features including some old glass, mainly heraldic with little shields in the upper lights, and the dining-room has some eighteenth-century panelling in a delightful pinkish colour, and a plaster ceiling of about 1600. It has some fine rococo mirrors between the windows, also original to this part of the house. There are two staircases; the one close to the dining-room is a newel stair in stone that gives access to the upper room in the oriel; the other which looks Queen Anne in date leads off behind the north-east corner of the hall. Between these two wings there appears no obvious way through at first-floor level, intriguing and in character with an old unplanned house, but not perhaps very convenient.

The gardens too are of interest – a ladies' flower garden to the north, and to the west a bowling green for the men (though ladies in their white summer hats now seem to be equally ardent practitioners of the game). There are a summerhouse and dovecot but the most striking feature, impossible to miss, is the enormous yew hedge which quite literally, one suspects, puts everything else in the shade! For age and survival it is unsurpassed.

Bingham's Melcombe may not be a house of the first rank of importance, but for its historic interest, its rambling charm and tranquil setting among the Dorset hills, it is surely one of the most lovable.

❧ BRYMPTON d'EVERCY

Somerset   *OS 183 519155*

The first sight of Brympton d'Evercy is unforgettable. Through gates between fine piers is a great and beautifully kept garden court, leading to the house; to the right the Chantry House, and close to that the small not quite cruciform church with its stumpy top-heavy belfry. Near to on the left is a late seventeenth-century stable block; closer to the house a curious little building in the Vanbrugh style – a garden house perhaps – and beyond that gardens rise steeply behind, now planted with vines. A lovely group, and all in gorgeous golden-yellow Ham Hill stone! What a picture!

There is no real village to speak of, and Brympton d'Evercy lies remote, approached by narrow lanes about half a mile to the south of the main road between Yeovil and Montacute. The Chantry House – or 'Dower' House – dates from the fifteenth century and adds enormously to the pleasure of the group. It has a staircase in a polygonal turret (now no longer in use since access to the building is through the shop at the other end) and this led to the Hall and Chamber above, a panelled room with a good fireplace and some simple traceried windows. In the Hall the owners, the indefatigable Mr. and Mrs. Charles Clive-Ponsonby-Fane, whose family* have been here since 1731, have mounted a compelling exhibition of their collective efforts to restore and run the house as private owners against what seem overwhelming financial odds. They appear billed as administrator, custodian, public relations officer, gardener, upholsterer and furnisher and their presentation focuses close attention on the burden and responsibilities of safeguarding a private house as part of the national heritage.

Of the west front the north end is the earliest and richest; it is early Tudor and really quite beautiful. The main part dates from about 1560 and the southern end, still too much hidden by a magnolia, is later. The projecting porch, 1722 Gothick with its jolly frieze and battlements, is by no means an unwelcome intruder and completes an eclectic if nevertheless very enjoyable façade.

The south front, set above a terrace, is entirely different, a superb sight, especially when seen from beyond the lake across the lawn. It is on a grand scale, but somewhat gauche and dates from the last years of the seventeenth century. It has ten bays and two storeys, with identical windows top and bottom, and alternating triangular and curved segmental pediments, starting with the curved below and the triangular above. This certainly gives a style, but ten bays does not make for strict symmetry and the whole composition requires the three down pipes, delightful with their leaded rainwater heads, to pull it together. The roof too has lost its stone slates, but the parapet is attractive. Altogether it is a façade of some presence and beauty, which a youthful creeper must never be allowed to hide.

Within, there is an Elizabethan fireplace in the hall, but the chief apartments are the state rooms on the south front, now delightfully furnished and lived in by the owners. Behind is a stately staircase which mounts in short flights with landings without changing direction until very nearly the first floor – architecturally a great extravagance! In one bedroom there were – and perhaps still are but the rooms upstairs are private – tapestries behind which the wall was just brick, neither plastered nor panelled for the tapestry was always to remain *in situ*. It is in many respects a puzzling house to read; at the back there is a projecting tower-like building with a staircase rising to two storeys and leading to nothing, and next to it another staircase, blocked. The problem of where the original hall was also lends itself to no easy solution.

Brympton d'Evercy is not quite one of the really great houses of England, but it is one of the most precious, and a house of considerable charm and distinction. 'There are greater, more historic, more architecturally impressive buildings in grander scenery' wrote Christopher Hussey 'but none of which the whole impression is more lovely. None that summarise so exquisitely English country life.'

* When he made his first visit, on 27 September 1947, Alec Clifton-Taylor was shown round by Mrs. Violet Clive, grandmother of the present owner. She had been described to him as 'a great eccentric'. She was indeed a remarkable woman who played hockey for the West of England, rowed for Leander and was an

excellent carpenter and gardener. She was somewhat 'casual of dress' and on numerous occasions apparently mistaken for one of the gardeners. 'I have three gardeners which is more than I can afford,' she said. 'My grandfather had fourteen and his wages bill was lower!' She herself created the part of the gardens to the north of the house, now a vineyard. She was somewhat dogmatic about dates and attributions and was at pains to point out how everything was 'skew-whiff', nothing at right angles or squared and the house full of architectural mysteries. When he called she was busy in the garden, but immediately gave up over an hour to show him round, even on to the roof – 'really very unselfish of her'.

Brympton d'Evercy

GARDEN PAVILION, MONTACUTE HOUSE

The house of Montacute, which takes its name from 'mons acutus', the steep cone-shaped hill that rises nearby to the west, is perhaps the Elizabethan house people love most; it is certainly a show-piece of the National Trust into whose hands it passed in 1931. It stands four miles west-north-west of Yeovil in a lovely village, all built of the local Ham Hill lias. It is England's most seductive stone, heavenly in colour and texture, honey-brown, cheesey-brown, whatever is your taste; it is delicious! Yet it may become brittle with age and splits and gives a good deal of trouble to the conservators.

Montacute dates from the last decade of the sixteenth century. The east side was once the entrance, and here the evidence of its period is most apparent: gables and obelisks, classical entablatures, columns for chimneys, and Nine Worthies in Norman dress in niches above. The west front is an addition of 1786 – but with a difference. The porch, a magnificent mixture of Gothic and the new fashionable Renaissance ornamentation imported from Europe, together with the buttresses and balustrade, all come from Clifton Maybank. This was a house in Dorset,* built about 1550 and then being demolished. The transplant works miraculously. The interior is marvellously kept and beautifully furnished, and the Long Gallery houses an excellent collection of sixteenth- and seventeenth-century portraits on loan from the National Portrait Gallery. There could be no more appropriate setting.

The gardens give great pleasure; to the north a central pool with Irish yew round three sides and a raised terrace at the perimeter, and to the south a huge bowling green and great yew hedge, but perhaps the garden of the east front (which is still the entrance for the public) is the most complete and of a piece with the house. It is one beautiful lawn enclosed by a wall with a balustrade and balusters of vertical symmetry, and this is surmounted by other adornments – obelisks, charming *tempietti* on either side (which however look a little top-heavy for comfort), and at the corners two stone pavilions or *plaisances*. These are summer houses; they are pure delight with their diamond leaded lights arranged diagonally to form a lattice pattern (well restored) and their ogee roofs are complete with lovely stone slates and finials.**

Montacute itself is glorious; its garden and the pavilions an especial joy.

* see also Bingham's Melcombe (p. 150)

** *Alec Clifton-Taylor loved gardens. He lived in South Kensington where he created a delightful garden, with a goldfish pond and an occasional visiting duck for company. He gardened a lot himself, and did as much of his writing as possible in the garden. He built too a garden room which was almost as good as being in the garden itself, and he kept a careful score of days spent there and in the garden, 'not in the house' to confound the more pessimistic critics of the English climate. In the north-west corner of the garden he had made to his design a garden shed in wood; a hexagon with ogee roof and finials.*

❧ LANHYDROCK GATEHOUSE

Lanhydrock, two and a half miles south of Bodmin, is beautifully situated in a fold of the hills on a slope which runs down to the River Fowey in the distance. The house which was for a long time in the ownership of the Robartes family was given to the National Trust in 1953. It is built, as to be expected in this part of Cornwall, of granite. Only three of the four sides of the original seventeenth-century house set round an inner courtyard survive, and they too only in a rebuilding of 1881 after a terrible fire. The fourth, a range to the east, was lost already by that time, so the house faces the morning sun. Some of the stonework on the south wing still looks unpleasantly new, and all the windows on this side and in the centre are now plain glass – a disastrous mistake where once all would have been leaded lights. What a wretched consequence of a rebuilding that had to come at such an unfortunate time, but luckily the north wing survived almost intact, and here is to be found the Long Gallery.

This Long Gallery is remarkable; one hundred and sixteen feet long, with a segmental arched ceiling, pendants at intervals and immensely elaborate plasterwork throughout its whole length with panels filled with Biblical scenes from the Old Testament – the Creation and so forth – decorated with flowers. On closer inspection the style is decidedly provincial and probably the work of the local North Devon plasterers, but the general effect is striking. The other rooms, although they convey much of the faded charms of life in the English country house at the turn of the century – smoking room, billiard room and considerable kitchens – are not of much account, though in some there are good miscellaneous pieces of furniture and furnishings, including writing tables, and tapestries from Brussels and Mortlake.

Lanhydrock is set in a fine park, and the formal gardens in front of the house were laid out in 1857 and are most appropriate: lovely lawns, with box hedges in a knot garden, rosebeds and pointed yews. The informal planting was mostly the work of Lord Clifden, the last of the Robartes line, in the 1930s. The gardens extend round the hillside from the church, small and much Victorianised, with a horrid reredos, but important in its grouping with the house. In full bloom these gardens are quite a sight: magnolia, copper beech, swamp cypress, azaleas and rhododendron.

In front of the courtyard a beautiful avenue of beech and sycamore, part of the planting by the first Lord Robartes in 1648, leads to a gatehouse, a charming frontispiece built about the same time and a few years after the original house. It is, like the house to which it is a herald, entirely symmetrical. It is extremely attractive and architecturally the best reason to visit Lanhydrock. It has two two-storeyed pentagons attached to either side of the gateway, and all the windows properly retain their leaded lights. Above the semi-circular arch there are some pleasantly articulated panels, and the battlement at the top bursts out in a flurry of little obelisks, a trifle too stunted perhaps, but complete with finial balls. Beyond, the long straight avenue recedes into woodland.

Great houses have their exits and their entrances, but there can be few that are as friendly or agreeable as this.

DUNDAS AQUEDUCT, LIMPLEY STOKE

Wiltshire

The hills that surround the valley of the Wiltshire Avon are full of stone – an oolitic limestone, not always a good one, known generally as Bath stone – but one that has stamped the character of the locality and provided a livelihood for those who worked it over many centuries. Many of the quarries and mines (for some are underground and quite shallow and honeycomb the hills) were close to or within reasonable distance of the river – at Corsham, Bradford-on-Avon, Westwood, Combe Down, Stoke Ground, Bathampton, to name but a few – and before the Industrial Revolution stone only travelled long distances by barge, so a waterway was vital. To meet this need the Kennet and Avon canal was opened in 1810. It was engineered by John Rennie, the Scottish architect whose work included bridges as far away as Lucknow and Naples, and who was to win fame with his Waterloo Bridge demolished to make way for the present one in 1938. The canal took sixteen years to build; it linked the valleys of the two rivers through a climb of nearly three hundred feet near Devizes with the famous ladder of twenty-nine locks (sixteen contiguous) at Caen Hill – pronounced Cane – within the space of two and a quarter miles. It thus made navigation possible, between London and Bristol through Reading and Bath, that is between the basin of the Thames and the Bristol Channel. This was one of the great canals of England. Bath stone could now go anywhere.

Between Bradford-on-Avon and Bath, the canal shared the valley with the river – and later with the railway which economically was soon to put it out of business – and on two occasions aqueducts had to be built to carry the canal across the river, one at Avoncliff, just below the Westwood mine (still going strong), and another near Limpley Stoke, not far from Stoke Ground. This is the Dundas aqueduct, designed by Rennie himself and built in 1795. It has three arches; the middle one is much the largest with a span of sixty-four and a half feet across the water, and tracks along the river bank below the steep wooded slopes of the valley pass through the arches to either side. When the railway arrived, a further lower arch had to be added to the west. The stone, or perhaps it was never more than stone facing, is ashlar and presumably from the local quarry. On the north face it is in decidedly poor condition (though not as bad as its companion at Avoncliff); it is patched in a shiny black blue-grey and pink brick,* colourful and well pointed, but certainly not right here, and the eastern arch has even suffered the humiliation of being rendered with cement.

It is, however, in the literal sense an aqueduct once more. For a long time the canal had fallen into disrepair; superhuman efforts organised by the Kennet and Avon Trust in recent years have raised money, fought for grants, cleared, drained, restored and rebuilt a new bottom, a task which involved much enthusiastic and energetic voluntary labour. It is now open again from Devizes to Bath. The Dundas aqueduct has become something of a marina, a lively scene and full of boats moored at the wharf. Now the water is flowing again – an obvious priority – it is profoundly to be hoped attention can focus on the stone. For this aqueduct with its fine voussoirs, its good Roman frieze and dentillation, with sturdy parapet and handsome balustrade, is both dignified and majestic; it is worthy of the most careful preservation.

* This seems a speciality of repair work on the canal; it crops up again at Avoncliff, Couch Lane Bridge at Devizes and elsewhere. It is absolutely wrong; entirely indefensible.

❦ STOURHEAD

Alec Clifton-Taylor wrote in his journals about Stourhead on two occasions – on a visit in 1950 with his sister Hazel, the dedicatee of The Pattern of English Building, *and with his mother, the co-dedicatee, two years later. He was devoted to both, but he appreciated the rare trees 'double as much through going round with Mother'.*

The little village of Stourton lies about four miles to the west of Mere, close to the watershed of the Dorset Stour, the Brue, which flows through Bruton into Somerset, and the Wylie which gives its name to Wiltshire. Here in the 1720s, Colen Campbell built Stourhead, a mansion in the Palladian style for the banker Henry Hoare, and within the next fifty years his son, of the same name, had transformed the scene, created the lake, and built the temples.

Stourhead is a sophisticated garden, subtle and really not at all 'natural'. But to an educated taste it is a paradise. The lake is extremely lovely, and in April there are countless thousands of daffodils and rhododendrons (first introduced here in 1791) already in bloom. In May it would be even better with azaleas, too, bluebells, and hundreds of fresh green trees, especially beech, all bursting forth. However, it is not for the flowers that you go to Stourhead. It is the landscape, and the little stone 'ornaments' which are the great attraction.

The effect is best appreciated, as was intended, if you walk down through the steeply-wooded slopes behind the house. Then the whole plan unfolds. Even if, somewhat mistakenly, you enter below, close by the village church and the much restored but happily sited Bristol Cross (early-fifteenth century in origin and re-moved here in 1765) the prospect is immediately enchanting. In the foreground is the five-arched bridge, and across the lake the dam; then as you move to the right, the Pantheon, the Rustic Cottage and the Grotto. Two other temples, Flora and Apollo, the latter perched upon the hill across the road to the left and affording a delicious view of the lake, complete the set.

Of all the ornaments, the Grotto is certainly the most exciting, with its startling lighting effects, and sparkle on the lake framed from within a dark cave. There are two sculptures, both in lead; Neptune, very effective, and the 'Nymph of the Grot', not specially good, reclining over a cascade of springs which flow continuously even in the driest of weathers. The floor is pebbled in pretty patterns, and on the pavement in front of the 'nymph' are carved two couplets by Pope – practitioner of garden design as well as a poet.

> 'Nymph of the Grot these sacred springs I keep
> And to the murmur of these waters sleep;
> Ah! spare my slumbers, gently tread the cave,
> And drink in silence or in silence lave.'

The Grotto is a complete success. Not so the Rustic Cottage: a sidelight on the eighteenth-century attitude to Gothic which was clearly regarded as quite primitive and fit only for rustics. It is amusing, with its pointed arches, quatrefoils and ogee on the bench outside, but in essence it remains a ridiculous object. The classical *tempietti* are infinitely to be preferred artistically and the Pantheon, finished in 1754 is a special delight. Like all the principal buildings it is by Henry Flitcroft, protégé of Lord Burlington, and it houses Rysbrach's magnificent marble Hercules of 1756 and his Flora of 1762.

The lake is surrounded by steep hills crowned in places with fine beeches, and there are many rare plants and trees,* best appreciated in the company of an expert. Nikolaus Pevsner regards Stourhead as second only to Stowe in its 'completeness and extent of layout and furnishing'. The total effect, while not the equal by any means of Pena Castle gardens at Cintra, is nevertheless strikingly beautiful, an infinite source of pleasure, with its delicate reflections in the lake, and, on a lucky day, puffy white clouds in a sky of blue. It is as Horace Walpole noted in 1762, 'one of the most picturesque scenes in the world'.

* The excellent guide to the ornaments and the planting, *The Stourhead Landscape*, by Kenneth Woodbridge, 1982, published by The National Trust, is greatly to be recommended; a complete guide to the planting is also published by The National Trust, *Mature Trees in the Stourhead Landscape*, 1981.

❀ CAMDEN CRESCENT, BATH

Somerset OS 172 747658

Many would regard Bath as the most beautiful city in England, and perhaps even in Europe. It is Palladian writ large, a triumph of elegance and proportion, urbane and polite, the spa beyond compare. It owes its rightful reputation to its historic Roman origin around the warm springs, to its wonderful hilly site which piles up terraces with a southern prospect unsurpassed in any town, to its satisfying sequences of fine houses and streets, squares, parades and crescents, culminating in the Circus and the famous Royal Crescent, the first in English architecture. It owes its character too, above all, to its being entirely built in one material – Bath stone.

Bath stone was known to the Romans, and as early as the ninth century was to be found as far away as Salisbury and London. From the quarry at Combe Down nearest the city, owned by Ralph Allen, who with Beau Nash and John Wood created the Georgian town, Bath was built. Bath stone is an oolite, excellent for decorative and ornamental work, but it is by no means impervious to rainwater (unless appropriately treated with a silicone repellent) and the ravages of weather and soot. It ranges in colour too; the delicate honey colour glows golden in the sun, whereas the more assertive yellows, to which the Victorians were so partial, can look a little harsh. It needs constant care and attention.

A series of fine terraces and villas fill steep slopes to the north of the city. Lansdown Crescent is perhaps the most celebrated; Somerset Place is nearly every bit as good, but Camden Crescent, a little off the beaten track to the east, deserves to be better regarded. It was built, in about 1788, for John Morgan, a carpenter and speculative builder, who engaged the services of John Eveleigh as architect. It is on a large scale, running from west to east and rising gently on a curve to a central feature, which has five giant columns supporting a pediment in which is the coat of arms of Lord Camden, after whom the crescent is named. It was never completed. There would have been twenty-eight bays on either side of the four at the centre (but to the east only thirteen were ever built) and that was not all. At either end (only that at the west was erected) were to be two straight flanking sections – 'book-ends' in effect – each of three bays with four columns, so in total this would have been a terrace or sixty-six bays with roughly one front door to every three bays.

There are some pretty balconies to the first floors, but they by no means survive with any regularity, and two giant creepers intrude; the one to the east is especially objectionable and it totally smothers the lower storeys of one whole house. The glazing bars too, as elsewhere in Bath, are incomplete. Only at the Circus and Laura Place – not even at the Royal Crescent – do they appear in anything like the manner they should. Three bays at Camden Crescent to the west have been well restored, but what a pity it is that arrangements could not be made at one and the same time for the whole, and that space for parked cars, always a blot, could not be found out of the way or round the back; the visual benefit would be immeasurable. Much of the fascination here admittedly lies in what might have been, and indeed what, with a good restoration, could be achieved. It is a most original and unconventional design, a little incomplete and unsophisticated perhaps, but nevertheless one of the delights of the city. To walk the terraces of Bath is a perambulation of the greatest pleasure, and Camden Crescent deserves to resume its rightful place *en route*.

THE EAST MIDLANDS

THE EAST MIDLANDS

BEDFORDSHIRE DERBYSHIRE LEICESTERSHIRE NORTHAMPTONSHIRE NOTTINGHAMSHIRE RUTLAND

Previous page: Staunton Harold Chapel

ST. MARY, EATON BRAY

Bedfordshire is not a county rich in stone for building; there is a little limestone to the north, but elsewhere it is mostly a coarse yellowy sandstone, flint and chalk. It is a chalk, mined at Totternhoe, a spur of the Chilterns on the outskirts of Dunstable, that gave the county some of its most notable buildings, and provided the stone at Eaton Bray, a village only a mile or so away. It has been variously described as hard chalk or soft limestone; it is usually grey or greenish white, but being soft, when used externally it weathers none too well. The effects can be seen at Eaton Bray; for while the grey colour of the stone is rather charming, the tower, somewhat stocky and overbuttressed with its 'Hertfordshire' spirelet clad in lead, has required some patching.

Within, it is a different story; the capabilities of this Totternhoe stone are seen to marvellous effect. The great thrill is the north arcade of the nave, one of the most exquisite examples of Early English on a small scale in England. The date is about 1235–40. There are five bays, and each of the piers is surrounded by eight shafts, of which the four facing the cardinal points of the compass are somewhat larger than the others. At the base there are well-defined mouldings, and at the top, crisply carved stiff-leaf capitals, all slightly different in design and of excellent quality

set between strong annulets – shaft-rings – and even stronger abaci above. The arches are most impressive with eleven rolls deeply cut and moulded, but seven centuries have taken their toll and they now lean worryingly out of plumb. The font like the capitals is carved with fine stiff-leaf and looks almost precisely contemporary. To the south the arcade, which is a little earlier, is much less interesting; here are stiff-leaf capitals above plain octagonal piers but it is still very respectable. This interior is whitewashed throughout, quite as the mediaevals would have wished (except there are no wall paintings). Whitewash may be particularly appropriate to a church, yet great care has to be taken with the carving lest there be a loss of crispness as a result. The south door, where the wood has been renewed, has some splendid thirteenth-century ironwork. Similar work can be seen at Leighton Buzzard and Turvey and almost certainly this came from the same workshop that produced Thomas de Leghtone, the smith famous for the railings around Queen Eleanor's monument in Westminster Abbey.

There are more interesting features to note; a good late Perpendicular reredos in stone, at the east end of the south aisle, and the east window, a Jesse window, with glass dated 1935 is quite attractive, especially from a distance. Happily the church has no bad glass. The chancel 'weeps' noticeably to the south, that is to the right as you look towards the altar.* On the west wall are two long hooked poles, one at least twenty feet long; they were for tearing off thatch if it caught fire, and their scorched ends bear evidence of their having been put, let it be hoped, to good effect.

In all this is a delightful, interesting and memorable interior; if St. Mary Astbury recalls King's College at Cambridge, here at Eaton Bray at the north arcade we have beauty little short of a Wells in miniature.

*In effect, as in many other parish churches, the chancel and nave are not aligned on the same axis. Alec Clifton-Taylor has an interesting, lengthy and not unamusing footnote on this in *English Parish Churches as Works of Art* (*op. cit.*) p. 204. There he refutes (and calls the authoritative H. Munro Cautley in evidence) any suggestions dear to the mystical musings of some clergy that this arrangement of the chancel was symbolic of the inclination of Christ's head upon the cross. The explanation lies simply in the rough and ready methods of early church-builders.

Opposite:
St. Mary, Eaton Bray:
left – the north arcade,
right – the south door

SOUTHWELL MINSTER

Nottinghamshire   *OS 120 702538*

Of all the English cathedrals Southwell is perhaps the least well known. This should not be so. It is a most lovable church, full of the choicest delights, and it stands in a small town of great charm, little more than the size of a large village. Of all England's Norman churches, it best preserves its original Romanesque aspect; a west front with twin towers of about 1140 – the large window was added later – and a third central tower, not a masterpiece but not unattractive, and a little like Tewkesbury though less rich and beautiful. Today only the two west towers, a restoration of 1880, have pyramidical 'snuffers', clad like all the roofs here in lead. They give the church a somewhat German appearance, and they lack a certain dignity: spires should be lofty or not exist at all.

Southwell takes a line of its own in quite a number of ways. The gables in the transepts have a pattern of zigzags with interstices all pierced with large dots; this is odd but quite striking and it makes for a nice texture. At the clerestory the windows look a bit like portholes of a liner, and the wavy corbel-table below the aisle roof is another curious feature. It is true that the Norman decoration, mainly zigzag with some billet, is repetitious and not at all inventive, and by Continental standards these outside elevations are excessively flat. Nevertheless despite its somewhat gawky and homespun appearance, the exterior at Southwell provides plenty to think about, and it is surrounded by a delightful, large, well-kept and spacious graveyard, with some pleasing Georgian houses close by. This would provide a real cathedral close if only the tombstones – and there are not so very many of them – could be cleared away. The best view of this Minster church, the only one apart from York, Ripon, Lincoln and Lichfield to have cathedral status, a distinction Southwell only achieved in 1884, is from the north-east, whence it composes beautifully.

The interior is far superior, and the stone particularly lovely. It is a 'white' Mansfield stone, quarried about fifteen miles away, a dolomitic sandstone in fact, although it contains a good deal of lime and many of the characteristics of that wonderful magnesian limestone from which York, Beverley and Selby, to name but three, were created. It is a delicious pale-honey colour and seems to hold the sunlight even when there is not much sun.

The nave is simple, dignified, and not at all heavy. It could be said it is too low and stylistically lacks dignity, and yet despite the inappropriate west window, which could with advantage take some good coloured glass, it is grand, restful and sure of itself. This interior is profound. At the crossing beneath the central tower the arches are splendid, lofty and strong, with bold cable mouldings. At the east and west they spring from multiform piers, which are to be preferred to the engaged circular piers at the north and south in the style of Gloucester. This is not a lantern tower and it has only a flat but barely noticeable wooden roof. The transepts are somewhat messy architecturally, especially the disposition of the windows at the

Opposite:
Southwell Minster:
south transept

172

two ends which are all over the place. In the north transept, at the north end of the west wall, is that strange and rather fascinating 'Urnes style' tympanum which shows Viking influence. The subject is St. Michael and the Dragon, rather a mixture stylistically and broken off at the left end, but clearly it has historical importance.

In churches of this size, the pulpitum – originally the word signified a platform or gallery on top of a screen and gives the word pulpit – serves to shut off the choir

Southwell Minster: Chapter House doorway

174

from the nave. Here at Southwell it has an enormous length of thirteen to fifteen feet, with vaulting underneath and flying ribs. The west side is more architectural perhaps, the east side much richer, sumptuous to a degree, a bit 'rank' and no doubt over-rich, yet the details are captivating, a wonderful *tour de force* of about 1320–30. There are dozens and dozens of little faces looking out from every level (no doubt a fair proportion Victorian restorations) and if it is overdone, it is overdone marvellously! This amazing pulpitum now has the misfortune to suffer the organ, the present one put here in 1934, smaller than its predecessor, but too big all the same. If fills almost the whole arch above and thereby interrupts (as it so lamentably often does in some of the loveliest of our churches) the view of the vault the whole length of the building from east to west. This organ should surely be relegated to the tribune where there is plenty of room for it; and the pulpitum have a simple cross in its place.

To pass through the pulpitum is to enter 'another world'. For some the choir will be too restless and a little fussy after the nave – 'stringy' is Pevsner's phrase – and although this is not Early English at its most pleasing, in many ways it is not uncharacteristic. For it does have considerable beauty, comparatively small in scale, and the vault with advantage could have 'sprung' a few feet higher up and risen to ten feet higher. Otherwise this two-storeyed design is a delight, reminiscent of Pershore, and has a great linear richness and a feeling of purity too.

Not all of course is as it should be. The ribbed vault has a not very attractive plaster infilling and the stained glass is mostly deplorable; even the sixteenth-

century French glass inserted in the lower four windows at the east end in 1818, though quite good in quality, is not right here. The eagle lectern (which looks about 1500 but is dated by a knowledgeable verger as 1408) is of solid brass and came from Newstead Priory where for two hundred years after the Dissolution it had reposed in the lake. For the most part the woodwork is modern and dull, but the misericords on the six canopied return stalls on the choir side of the pulpitum are quite splendid. They are in fine condition, contemporary with the pulpitum itself and have magnificent undercutting with some interesting subjects; Samson on a lion, a pair of lovers, a curious bird man, and a 'Green Man' – the 'tree-spirit' of traditional mediaeval ceremony and undoubtedly pagan origin, who was paraded through the fields to encourage fertility. His heyday is commemorated in the naming of many an English inn.

The two bays at the east end where the sanctuary now is once formed a separate chapel behind the high altar, as at most other cathedrals, and an ambulatory went across linking the two east bays of the choir aisles where there are now steps. At Southwell this was never a Lady Chapel, as the Minster was itself dedicated to St. Mary the Virgin and this was probably therefore a Jesus Chapel.

To say 'Southwell', however, is to mean the Chapter House, a miracle of carved ornamentation. It is octagonal, only thirty-one feet in diameter, and by comparison with Salisbury or Westminster only half their size. Because of this there is no central pier and this makes possible a glorious star-vault. The key to this marvellous Chapter House is the Mansfield stone; it is fine in grain and cuts very smoothly, and

Southwell Minster: The 'Leaves of Southwell'

176

here in the hands of some wonderful carvers we have ornament in profusion – the renowned 'Leaves of Southwell' which adorn the wall arcades of the vestibule, the superb double-arched doorway with its slender polygonal pier, and the capitals and gables above the thirty-six stalls in the Chapter House itself.

This is nature abundant, oak, hop, hawthorn, wild apple, wild rose, white bryony, the ivy and the vine, potentilla and buttercup. Such is the precision and detail in the depth and texture of the undercutting that you imagine these sculptors must have brought back freshly-gathered bundles from the neighbouring fields as models. In the proper cause of artistic unity all the leaves are carved to the same scale – which is not as they are in nature – so that the small leaf of the hawthorn and the large leaf of the ivy appear the same size. The master-carver – and there were probably two others at least besides – had, it seems, and not surprisingly, a special place of prominence, at the central shaft of the doorway. His theme was the buttercup, sprouting and bursting into life. Leaves predominate but there are a few flowers, and even some faces; a self-portrait of the master-carver himself, perhaps, appears at a corbel on one of the gables of the stalls, and above the hawthorn capital the Green Man is again in evidence.

There are three styles to be distinguished here, probably explained by the differing ages of the masons. The first and much the least important is the hangover from the Early English, with foliage of a conventional type, still reminiscent of stiff-leaf and no particular leaf specified. Then the fully naturalistic style, which nevertheless is not just copying. 'It has a soul,' says Pevsner, 'and does not only please the senses . . . the carvers were never satisfied with mere imitation but succeeded in keeping stone as stone, in preserving intact the smoothness and firmness of surfaces; in short they achieved a synthesis of nature and style.' This is Southwell at its supreme, and aesthetically the best. Lastly there is much work closer to the later Decorated 'knobbly' style – more generalised, more impressionistic and less 'individual' leaf by leaf. In the end this becomes inferior, notably in the rather seaweedy-looking leaves (could they be acanthus?) on the upper sides of the gables above the stalls. The carvings within the gables are also more generalised and less articulated; it is aesthetically a change for the worse. The central boss in the Chapter House probably belongs to this group (and if so it is the style at its best) – the work of a younger carver just as the building was being completed about 1300. It is full of joy and gives great delight, but it foreshadows a move away again from nature to a more standardised all-over pattern rather than of individual species – and this in the end was to produce the four-leaved flower of the Perpendicular period which could be so mechanical and unattractive.

Some observers have perceived at Southwell a decline in artistry from the flair of imagination and fantasy that impregnated Romanesque at its (all too rare) best. That is probably true. The leaves of Southwell may not be in intellectual terms as fine as the best of the capitals in the Canterbury crypt, but to enjoy the carving at Southwell is to wonder at its creators' feeling for decoration and the emulation of the natural world they saw around them; it is to admire the supreme precision and detail of their skill and to rejoice in the uplift of spirit in their achievement.

❧ SOMERSAL HALL

Derbyshire OS 128 137352

Somersal Herbert – 'Somershall', the old spelling on the map is apparently no longer correct – lies four miles east-north-east of Uttoxeter, and is a remote village, off the beaten track and in a dip. Unusually for Derbyshire the Hall which faces north, is half-timbered – but what a picture! Calculated asymmetry, with overhang and four gables, only the two smallest of which are set at the same height! The oak is a lovely silvery brown, with quite a lot of decoration in the gables, and the infilling is fawn, which is a most appropriate colour if slightly too 'cementy'. Two tablets at the entrance date the building as 1564, but, as to be expected, much has been added over the years. To the back, the garden front on the south side is partly Georgian and the Victorian additions, to the east and at the porch, are a pity but at least they do not impinge too much. The chimney-stacks are modern too, fairly plain and in red brick. The oval lawn in front is just right, but has mistakenly been planted recently with shrubs and saplings which will one day, no doubt as intended, hide the house. This may be good for privacy perhaps, but it does not suit the approach and will sadly deprive the casual passer-by or visitor to the churchyard of a very enjoyable *bonne bouche* along their route!

✿ ST. GUTHLAC, PASSENHAM

Northamptonshire

'Ham', ubiquitous in English place-names, means a meadow, especially by water, and considering the encroachments of Milton Keynes are only but a few miles away to the south, it is difficult to imagine anything more remote or pastoral than Passenham, approached down a narrow lane over an even narrower bridge across the Great Ouse. The settlement is pre-Conquest; Passa was a Saxon settler, and the dedication, one of only about ten in England, is to St. Guthlac, soldier in the army of King Ethelred of Mercia who later took against strong drink, embraced a life of austerity, and lived the life of a hermit on the River Welland in the Fens.

On the outside the church, except for its delightful grouping beside the walled and moated Passenham Manor, is not particularly notable. It is built of a rubbly buff-coloured limestone, once clearly roughcast, although the chancel is ashlar with a curved roof of lead. The interior is, however, quite remarkable. It owes its survival in the first place and its most important embellishment to Sir Robert Banastre who rebuilt the chancel in 1626. He was Lord of the Manor for forty years, Comptroller of the Household to James I and if local ghost stories have any credence, a villain of some notoriety as well as benefactor.

First the woodwork; it is most enjoyable. There are fourteen lovely oak stalls and two returns with fine mouldings and much refinement, dated 1628. The misericords, which are carved with considerable sophistication and mastery, include several large heads, a lion, a bull, a unicorn, a fox and a dragon. The pulpit with its large tester, probably reconstructed about 1800 from a Jacobean predecessor, is another delight. It is beautifully carved in oak, and benefits enormously from having its brown varnish removed and a few details picked out in red, blue and gold. Likewise the box pews and panelling have been tastefully repainted; here the scheme is olive-grey-green with white relief. The west gallery is borne on four Ionic columns, and has a most extraordinary carved frieze, purely pagan in character and Renaissance in style. It is just possible, but it seems unlikely, that this may once have been part of a rood screen, but why should it not always have been where it is now?

The great surprise is the wall paintings, also dated 1626, which surround the chancel above the canopies of the stalls. From north-west to south-east they represent the four major prophets, Isaiah, Jeremiah, Ezekiel and Daniel; at the east Nicodemus and Joseph of Arimathea carrying the dead Christ; and on the south, Matthew, Luke and John. Mark was almost blotted out as early as 1650 by the Banastre monument. John is not well preserved, and Matthew and Christ have lost their faces.

Yet what we see is all the work of a most thorough restoration carried out with consummate skill and care in 1962–6 at the expense of the Pilgrim Trust by E. Clive Rouse. The whole decorative scheme was revealed by him and then reconstituted with the help of his assistant, Ann Ballantyne. The figures are fully life-size, in the Venetian late Cinquecento style and set in shell-headed niches within an architectural framework in *trompe l'oeil*. They are frescoes, that is paint applied direct to wet plaster while it is still 'fresh', and while by no means masterly (they are indeed decidedly provincial) the colours are very pleasing and they are the most distinguished of any post-Reformation wall painting, in English parish churches. The rediscovery of these murals in the early 1950s, hidden for the last two centuries, was a most extraordinary piece of good fortune; we should be doubly grateful that their restoration has been one of such sensitivity and respect. The paintings do not *look* restored, and indeed the restoration is not complete – witness John not well 'preserved' and the faceless Matthew and Christ. It is all so skilful that it begs the question as to how much is reliable restoration and how much inspired guesswork!

There are good stone floors everywhere. The only blot is the stained glass – two overbright windows in the manner of Evans of Shrewsbury and a later Victorian east window which is a brute. This exquisite church ill deserves such assertive bad taste. Fortunately there are six windows of clear glass, and long may they remain so! Passenham is quite difficult to find, and the church, sadly of necessity like so many others has to be kept locked. Directions how to find the key are given clearly. It will unlock a richly rewarding interior, well worth every effort to see.

ARCHBISHOP CHICHELE'S SCHOOL, HIGHAM FERRERS

Northamptonshire   *OS 153 963686*

Higham Ferrers, a charming small town five miles east of Wellingborough, all built in the agreeable local limestone has a fascinating ecclesiastical enclave, clustered together just east of the main street: church, hospital and Archbishop's School. The church of St. Mary is large, Early English and Decorated and among the finest in the county. It has quite a robust tower, the upper stages of which together with the spire had to be rebuilt after collapsing in the 1630s. The spire is a beauty, crocketed, and linked to the corner turrets of the tower by little flying buttresses pierced with quatrefoils. It has three tiers of spire lights in the usual Northamptonshire style. The west door, a double door, is inside a porch and has a carved tympanum, dating from about 1250. It has ten roundels, some cut off by the curve of the arch, with familiar scenes such as the Three Magi, the Crucifixion and the Harrowing of Hell. These surround the central theme of the Jesse tree the stem of which rises to support a modern image of Mary and Child which is white and not good against the grey limestone. The roundels are elaborate, and surprisingly escaped the attentions of the iconoclasts, but they are badly weathered, not a satisfying composition, and despite the historic interest this is a minor work of art.

The interior of the church is really rather impressive, but it is not helped by dark oak pews and some dull Victorian glass and two quite lamentable recent windows. There are some famous brasses, which, if you like brasses, are especially good and the one of Laurence St. Maur, a priest who died in 1337, is among the finest in the country. The set of twenty original collegiate stalls in the chancel have great appeal; their misericords, if a little on the dark side, are particularly fine for a parish church, bold, lively and varied; mostly heads and some animals, the lion, and familiar pelican. But the most pleasure is to be derived from the exceptionally fine Decorated window tracery, best seen from outside. At the east end of the chancel and adjacent to the Lady chapel there are two large reticulated windows with a net-like effect of circles and ogee shapes, typical of the early fourteenth century. Three more appear on the south side of the chancel and one on the north side, not reticulated, but quite lovely. All these windows are under swinging ogee arches, with the two at the east having attractive little niches above the points of the 'canopies'; these are perhaps among the best reticulated windows in England.

Archbishop Chichele, founder of All Souls', Oxford, and a benefactor who endowed a number of professorial chairs, was born in Higham Ferrers in about 1362. His portrait appears with two clerks on the Master's and Vicar's stall in the church. Here he founded – or refounded for they were already established – the Bede House, a hospital or almshouse which lies to the south and the Chantry chapel which had existed as a school in the late fourteenth century. The Bede House, 1428, is a long hall which was divided into cubicles to accommodate twelve elderly men

looked after by a woman attendant. At the east end, on what is now the platform of the parish hall (for this building has found a good modern use) was formerly a raised chapel. The Bede House has layers of ironstone and white limestone and looks not unlike a multi-decker sandwich – it is not unattractive, but is marred by having a relentlessly regular red roof of machine-made tiles.

Higham Ferrers is blessed with treasures, but the finest is undoubtedly the Archbishop's School which dates from six years earlier than the Bede House and is unspoiled in its loveliness. Its special feature is a most beautiful Perpendicular pierced parapet above a string course, punctuated by crocketed finials. For three hundred years it contained a schoolroom, but in 1945 was restored to its original use. It is a miniature of exquisite delight.

❧ OLD GRAMMAR SCHOOL, APPLEBY PARVA

Leicestershire   *OS 128 308088*

Few children under the age of eleven can have such an imposing building in which to start their school days, for the Old Grammar School at Appleby Parva, as distinct from Appleby Magna where the church and manor are to be found, is now the Church of England Primary school, named after the benefactor of the earlier foundation, Sir John Moore. He was a grocer and Lord Mayor of London. No less an architect than Sir Christopher Wren had designed for him at Christ's Hospital, and it was to him again that he originally turned for his school at Appleby Parva. Plans under his guidance were drawn up by Thomas Woodstock, who had worked as a carpenter on some of the city churches. On Woodstock's death, Sir William Wilson (*ibid* Sudbury Hall) whom Moore believed 'to be an ingenious gentleman', took over as Surveyor. He drastically altered the designs and claimed this had Wren's approval. Wilson's school wears a Jacobean air; it cost far more than Sir John Moore had anticipated, but it is without doubt a splendid building, and Wilson at his best. The date is 1693–7.

The appeal lies mainly in the materials. The mellow pink brick is superb and the handsome mullion and transom windows with straightforward moulded frames of stone nearly all retain their leaded diamond panes. The school is built on an H-plan, and at the centre, above the five arched loggia which acts as an open arcade, is the main schoolroom, and in it a bust of the founder by Wilson, who had started life as a mason and carver. On either side are the English and Writing schools, and above, at attic level there is a dormitory still divided by boarders' cubicles. The roof has a charming lantern capped in lead with a delightful weathercock on top. To the west, for this is a north face, is a Victorian addition, the Headmaster's house, much in the style of the main building and not at all bad in its own right, an excellent example of an architectural good neighbour.

The Old Grammar School is a very happy composition. Moreover it has dignity and calm well suited to its purpose: a proper place for the pursuit of godliness and sound learning.

185

WILLINGTON DOVECOT

Bedfordshire OS 153 106500

The village of Willington lies four miles east of Bedford, north of the main road to Sandy, and remote. Here in the 1530s, John Gostwick, a rich man of yeoman stock who had come up in the world first in the service of Cardinal Wolsey, to whom he became Master of the Horse, and then of Henry VIII, built himself a manor house. Bedfordshire is not well endowed with stone, and so it was in brick. About ten years later when he turned his hand to extend the estate with a barn, a stable and a dovecot, the nearby Newnham Priory had been dissolved. Gostwick was himself treasurer of some of the monastic revenues that now accrued to the Crown, and the priory had of course been built in stone.

So stone was used for the dovecot, albeit a rather rubbly one, where usually half timber and brick would suffice for such a building of fairly humble requirement and pretence. Willington dovecot is one of the largest of its kind. It must be over seventy feet high and its odd stepped gables, which accommodate the two roofs and slatted wood louvres between them for birds to fly in and out, dominate the flat landscape for miles around. There are two chambers, and fifteen hundred nesting boxes. In some smaller circular dovecots, these were serviced by a 'potence' (from the French 'gallows'), that is a ladder mounted at the end of a beam which stemmed horizontally from a central pivot, like a spoke from the hub of a wheel. This enabled the keeper to move freely round the nests. Willington lent itself less easily to such an ingenious device; tall and oblong, and on this grand scale, it was surely built as much to impress as to provide convenience for keepers or comfort for cooing doves!

In the nineteenth century, after the estate had been in the hands of the Dukes of Bedford for over a hundred years, a steward with a keen eye for more up-to-date economic management determined on demolition. This caused more than a flutter in the dovecot; the Bedfordshire Archaeological Society made representations and His Grace reprieved the dovecot and stable. What a blessing! Both buildings passed into the hands of the National Trust in 1914 and are now safe from the assaults of economic husbandry.

Opposite:
Willington Dovecot

STAUNTON HAROLD CHAPEL

Leicestershire OS 128 380209

Staunton Harold is unforgettable. The chapel, house, lakes fringed with great cedars, and meadows grazed by cattle are the quintessence of what it feels to be in England. There is much interest too, and many a delight: interest because this is one of the very few churches – it was never parochial and served as the private chapel of the great house – to be built in England during the Common-wealth. The famous inscription over the west door tells the tale: 'when all thinges

Sacred were throughout ye nation Either demollisht or profaned Sir Robert Shirley, Barronet, Founded this church'. The date is 1653, four years after the execution of King Charles I. Cromwell was furious; if a man had money for a church, he could raise a regiment. Sir Robert, staunchly Royalist, refused. Within three years, he died in the Tower, aged twenty-seven.

The chapel, dedicated to the Holy Trinity, is his memorial, and its great beauty lies in its complete unity; it is entire. Everything except the poor Victorian window at the east is appropriate, and even the six aisle windows of about 1900, though not good do not detract from the harmony of the interior. From a distance the church looks wholly mediaeval; Perpendicular in grey stone with low pitched roofs, embattled parapets, a Decorated east window, and a beautiful tower, massive and just the right height, with a handsome crown, worthy of Somerset.* Four gilded weather-vanes top the corner pinnacles. All this then appears Gothic, but the west end, ornate with pilasters, angels and drapes betrays the date, the final flourish of 1662–5 when the master mason Richard Shepheard completed the building.

Within, Gothic plays host to Jacobean; there is a wealth of wonderful seventeenth-century woodwork, with panelling on the walls and around octagonal piers, all oak, not too dark, and even on a winter's day really very cosy! There are box pews, always a help to keep out draughts, complete with brass candlesticks. High up in the west gallery – and how rare it is to say this of an English church – is a charming

Staunton Harold Chapel and Hall

little organ, dated 1686. The *pièce de résistance*, however, though later than Sir Robert's furnishings and reflective of a more sophisticated taste, is the magnificent wrought-iron chancel screen. It is a delightful work of art, black with happily subdued highlights in gold, surmounted with a coat of arms, and it is of superb craftsmanship, of about 1711 and probably the work of Robert Bakewell of Derby. The ceiling paintings, by S. and Z. Kyrk, are not of a quality comparable with the rest of the decorations of the church and are best forgotten.

The hall lies adjacent to the chapel, and had been empty for ten years and semi-derelict when it became a Cheshire Home in 1955. To that admirable organisation we owe a great debt of gratitude, not only for its restoration but for its being put to an excellent modern use. The house is mainly of 1760, built of brick with stone dressings, and the three central bays of its quite imposing eleven-bay front are faced with ashlar. Within there are some pleasing items, but the best feature is the great staircase, now well restored, with three cantilevered flights of stone stairs and a beautiful balustrade of wrought iron. It is a simple, dignified house, and not without interest, but admittedly it does not inspire. The delight of Staunton Harold lies essentially in its grouping and its setting, and the chapel of the Holy Trinity is a major pleasure.

*See p. 136 for Somerset Towers.

Staunton Harold
Chapel: interior

Alec Clifton-Taylor visited Sudbury Hall three times and twice wrote extensive notes. On 11 September 1951 his enthusiasm was somewhat muted; on 15 August 1973 the superlatives flowed free. The transformation was occasioned almost entirely by the restorations carried out by the National Trust during 1967–70. It was mostly the work of John Fowler, although many were consulted, including James Lees-Milne. The earlier slight disappointment gave way to two hours' unending pleasure.

The old idea to which Christopher Hussey subscribed, that the shell of Sudbury Hall was a Jacobean house of about 1620 left unfinished is now considered erroneous. It is broadly agreed that the house dates substantially from the 1660s and that it is largely the creation of George Vernon, who inherited the estates in 1659 and was squire until 1702, though whether he acted as his own architect and surveyor is still open to debate.*

The house faces north-east and stands quite close to what was once the main road. There is now, thank goodness, a by-pass, and even this was sunk where it passed nearby, so Sudbury Hall enjoys the best of both worlds. It has an E-shaped plan, on traditional Elizabethan-Jacobean lines, and is sited graciously beyond a broad green lawn. The material is a red brick with blue diapers, not, it is true, an attractive brick, but it is well served with stone dressings. The single most striking external feature is the stone cupola but the roof itself is difficult to assess since it was much altered in 1872 when a top balustrade was removed, and the present one above the cornice appeared. The windows are not particularly appealing; they tend to be rather too large and severely plain. For the most part they are mullioned and transomed, but to the left and right of the central porch – and again at either end of the Long Gallery to the rear, a singularly ugly design occurs of two round-headed windows with an oval above. This must be the work, as indeed was the porch itself, of Sir William Wilson. He was the son of a Leicestershire baker; his apprenticeship was as a statuary mason, and he undoubtedly improved his prospects under the influence of a rich widow whom he later married. He also became a Freemason. His talents were not, it must be said, among the foremost of his contemporaries; he was responsible for the rebuilding of the nave at St. Mary, Warwick, and there his window motif, though on a grander scale, recurs to hideous effect. He was not knighted for his architectural achievements. His somewhat elaborate and cumbersome Baroque frontispiece for Sudbury may have been an innovative style there, but it was already out of date in the wider world of architectural taste.

If in some respects, therefore, this exterior is disappointing and even a little *retardatif*, this is certainly not true of the internal arrangements. Here Vernon was extremely up-to-date and chose his craftsmen with confidence and masterly assurance. One of the chief glories is the staircase in the north corner of the house. The scale is magnificent. If for some it is a little heavy, the proportions justify the heaviness; majestic is the only word. The stairs float in space without visible support. The craftsmanship is brilliant; cornucopia is the theme: the acanthus, first and foremost appears at the balustrade, and large rosettes, swags of fruit, seed pods bursting open, and baskets of flowers and fruit embellish the newel posts. Where once the wood was dark brown, it is now properly, and with great benefit, painted white. The carver was Edward Pierce (some spellings have it 'Peirce') from London, best known for his fine portrait busts of Wren and Oliver Cromwell now in the Ashmolean Museum at Oxford. High above, and also below the landing and the underside of the staircase, there is some gorgeous plasterwork of amazing skill by another Londoner, James Pettifer. Only the paintings of Louis Laguerre, called in about 1695 as a leading practitioner of the Baroque mural, detract from the overall pleasure of this marvellous sight.

There is more superb plasterwork by Pettifer (who was concerned also with some of the stucco for the City churches, then rebuilding) in the Saloon which has Pierce carving at the wainscot, some giltwood chandeliers, and gilded lead wall brackets – quite a sumptuous collection. Here as in the Drawing Room his partner was Robert Bradbury, and the restorations, wonderfully executed, reveal their achievements as the splendid works of art they are. The ceiling in the Drawing

Room has been most beautifully painted in white against a background of very pale grey-pink and a stronger grey. This room had been thrown into one by Salvin in a restoration of about 1850 when he contemplated another Harlaxton – which here would have been disastrous. The National Trust wisely reverted to the original plan, and here is to be seen the great treasure of the house: an early and quite superb work in limewood by Grinling Gibbons, executed in 1678 at a cost of £40, in the shape of a surround for a picture over the fireplace with sporting motifs. It is exquisite. In the Library the ceiling is more modest but nevertheless still a delight – the work by Samuel Mansfield – although the black and white chimney-piece seems strangely out of place among all this dignity and style.

And so to the Long Gallery, which runs the length of the garden front to the south-west, one hundred and thirty-eight feet two inches long. Such a gallery was a great feature of the Elizabethan and Jacobean period, but by 1660 it was already out of fashion. If then it was Vernon's fancy, how grateful we should be! On a good day it is sunny, and it too has a showpiece Bradbury ceiling, completed in 1760, white on a background of pale buff with a carved cornice on a ground of pale grey-pink like the panelling. The side away from the windows used to be lined with books, as always no doubt only for decorative purposes; nowadays portraits are hung to great advantage. Some connoisseurs have adversely criticised this ceiling with its

wreaths of oak-leaves and flowers within geometrical plaster panels as too repetitive, but the frieze with garlands, scallops in shells, palm branches and Roman heads is surely most effective and much to be admired.

In the gardens to the south-west the lake had been cleared and there are acres of lovely mown grass. To the north is a deer park with a deercot of about the middle of the eighteenth century. It is a real eye-catcher, one of the largest it is said in existence, and it incorporates a sham gatehouse resembling a child's toy fort, complete with turrets. Sudbury Hall is superb. With his skill in knowing how to

use his money and to choose the best and most sophisticated craftsmen of his day, George Vernon not only did himself proud; he also provided an interior of supreme delight which could be a cause of wonder for generations of visitors to come.

*John Cornforth persuasively argued that Vernon was responsible for the whole house; *Country Life*, vol. 149, 1971, pp. 1428–33. H.M. Colvin has his doubts. For an excellent and illuminating summary see *The Buildings of England: Derbyshire*, Nikolaus Pevsner rev. Elizabeth Williamson, Penguin, 1979, pp. 332–333.

BURLEY HOUSE GATES

Rutland *OS 130 884104*

'The best things come in smallest parcels: Rutland is both very small and very good.' So wrote Dr. W.G. Hoskins in his splendid short guide; Dr. Pevsner said his words could not be improved, and he was glad to copy them and said so.* Rutland was the smallest of English counties by far in comparison with any other, but in 1974 it became, much to the sorrow not only of its locals but many others the length and breadth of the kingdom, a district of Leicestershire. Nevertheless it has retained its own marked individuality, helped in no small measure by its two principal limestones which provide the materials for building and which are the envy of many other counties much larger. To the west is the Lias, a rich golden brown, which because of its iron oxide content is sometimes referred to as ironstone, and to the east the prestigious oolite of Great Casterton, Ketton and Clipsham. The great house at Burley-on-the-Hill boasts two of them; Clipsham at the centre over a brick core, and a colonnade of Ketton. It has a wonderful site, and there is a stunning view from the Oakham to Stamford road a mile to the south.

Here for once however it is neither the stone nor the house that commands attention, but the wrought-iron gates that guard the entrance to the vast courtyard before it. The craftsmanship is superb. Between 1690 and 1750 wrought iron was much in vogue for staircases and balconies in great houses, screens in churches, gates and railings in formal gardens. The ideal setting was always the garden though a considerable number were swept aside with the art of the landscape gardener who not only destroyed many but reduced the demand for more. There are, however, some marvellous survivors; the works of the great Tijou at Burghley and Hampton Court, Robert Bakewell at Derby Cathedral, the Warren family at Cambridge, and that ascribed to William Edney at Scraptoft Hall not far away in Leicestershire. Here at Burley the work is by the otherwise unknown Joshua Lord, and is dated 1705. His gates are the single most important feature of the house; they are magnificent and *obligatoire*.

Opposite: Burley House Gates

**The Buildings of England: Leicestershire and Rutland*, Nikolaus Pevsner rev. Elizabeth Williamson, Penguin Books, 1984, p. 433.

ROCKINGHAM

Northamptonshire   *OS 141 866918*

The castle built by William the Conqueror dominates the village of Rockingham. It was an admirable choice of site, on a spur of high ground commanding the valley of the Welland, and from it extend wide views of what were until 1974 at least five counties, and, less attractively, the encroachment of Corby, immediately to the south. Not much remains of the Norman castle except the keep and gateway, but two comfortable houses were created here in the sixteenth century when Edward Watson obtained a lease from the crown in 1553.

The great attraction of Rockingham, however, lies in the enchanting village itself, strung out along a main road at the foot of the hill and beset all too often with thunderous juggernauts, but accurately described in the words of the old Collins Guide 'the Dunster of the Midlands'. The cottages mostly date from the seventeenth and eighteenth centuries, and all are built of a golden-brown ironstone, for Rockingham is right on the limestone belt and had its own quarry in the village, with many others within four or five miles. Here it is a rubblestone, perfectly appropriate for the humbler dwellings of a village, particularly when, as is seen to perfection in Rockingham, the dressings are of ashlar.

Rockingham also shows some of the finest thatch in the county, a wheat straw, as soft as velvet, sometimes fancifully shaped – one example even has an inverted ogee arch – at the ridge. The thatching has, moreover, a decided stylistic unity, and this is usually evidence of the work of a single thatcher or family traditional to the area, or the ownership of a single landowner, such as a 'feudal' village like Rockingham. The threat to the survival of thatch comes not from a lack of thatchers – for there are many who want to work here in this locality – but a shortage of long enough lengths of wheat straw, strains of which are no longer grown; and those which are, in these mechanical days, are bruised and crushed by the combine harvester. Norfolk reed is a good, durable and acceptable substitute, but it is decidedly second-best. Other cottages have Collyweston stone slates – from the famous mines only fifteen miles to the north-east, and these, on a shallower pitch make a no less lovely roof. Even the telephone and electric wires have been carefully taken behind the cottages well away from sight. One day too, no doubt, a tidier though still efficient arrangement for television aerials will become more readily available. Rockingham is a delight, a gem of a village.

Rockingham

THE STABLES, CHATSWORTH

Derbyshire OS 119 263703

Chatsworth, built for the first Duke of Devonshire by Talman between 1687 and 1707, must be among the best documented of all the grand English country houses. There is so much to see, pictures, drawings, books and furniture, and an enormous garden, and so much to read about that a visitor may well be forgiven for feeling too exhausted for the extras. But do not on any account miss the stables. They are first-rate and of Brobdingnagian proportions.

The stables lie to the north-east of the house, close to Wyattville's north wing, and are built on a quadrangular pattern of the same dun-coloured, neutral tinted stone as the house – probably a millstone grit. They were built for the fourth duke in 1758–63 by James Paine; robust, handsome, with a magnificent triumphal-arch and coat of arms in the pediment, and surmounted by a clock-tower with an open cupola. The extraordinary feature is the Cyclopean rustication on the columns; gaiters indeed for a giant. This is no sideshow; the stables have strong personality, worthy of a duke, and fit for his horse!

Below:
Chatsworth Stables

✻ MONTAGU HOSPITAL, WEEKLEY

Northamptonshire

Weekley is now almost submerged by Kettering, but like its neighbour Warkton, it really lies within the shadow of the great house at Boughton, which is only a mile away across the park to the north-east, the historic home of Wentworth and Montagu. In 1611 Sir Edward Montagu built and endowed his hospital of that name for a master and six brethren, old retainers from his estate. It was a small foundation in comparison with others of his day. It is charming, handsome in its grey ashlar, lovable and easy on the eye with its windows widely spaced and mullioned. The centre piece above the entrance is somewhat capricious, but no less enjoyable for that. Obelisks abound – two on shells which flank the coat of arms, and three at the jaunty bulbous-shaped gable above. Obelisks apparently were a favourite family motif for they turn up too on the Montagu family monument in the church. A large sundial, always assuming the sun was shining, marks the time of passing day.* The years too move on; the hospital is no longer able to fulfil the intention of its founder, presumably because of a combination of economic stringency and the standards now quite properly expected in care for the elderly. In 1972 it became a private house, and it looks much cherished and in good hands. Successors to a long and honoured tradition – and what lucky people.

Opposite:
Chatsworth

*The sundial has the words from Ovid, *Fasti VI*, 771: 'Tempora labuntur tacitisque senescimus annis' – Time slips by and we grow old with the silent years.

Montagu Hospital,
Weekley

DERBY CATHEDRAL

Derbyshire

Derby has a cathedral only in name; the chief parish church of the town, dedicated to All Saints, which could trace a foundation back to before the Norman conquest, was raised to cathedral rank only in 1927. In effect it is a large preaching hall designed by James Gibbs in 1723–5 and tacked on to a tall late Perpendicular tower built two centuries earlier. The stone is not limestone, but either a grit or sandstone, and if it is allowed too long to fall prey to the weather and the smoke it can become very dirty and dour and even unstable. It needs regular cleaning.

The tower with its lofty pinnacles rises to over two hundred feet, and replaces an older one demolished in about 1475. It was begun in 1520 and took twelve years to build. It is fine in outline, but does not improve on closer inspection; the details are coarse and the design rather uninspired. The master mason was John Otes who had worked as mason-setter with the famous John Wastell at King's College, Cambridge.

By contrast with the height of the tower, the church is somewhat squat, and intentionally so, said Gibbs, on grounds of expense and suitability with the 'old steeple' (did the tower then have a spire?) and the exterior is said to be a mixture of the first design for St. Mary-le-Strand, and an early rejected design for St. Martin-in-the-Fields. The interior is wide and spacious and not marred by galleries but it can hardly be called beautiful.

Gibbs' furnishings disappeared in a restoration by Temple Moore in the first few years of this century. From the Gibbs' building one outstanding feature survives, the most lovely wrought-iron screens, beautifully painted in dark blue and gold which run the whole width of the church. They are superb. This is the work of Robert Bakewell, a wonderful local craftsman who may also have been responsible for Staunton Harold, and who died in 1752. The communion rails, the mace stand and support for the altar in the south chapel are also his, along with the railings which surround the monument to Thomas Chambers by Roubiliac. Two parclose screens of simpler design at right angles on either side of the chancel were assembled about 1900.

The divide between nave and chancel (especially in a mediaeval church with a fine vault and vista the length of the church) is visually a most sensitive area. Organ cases, for example, should never, in any circumstances, be tolerated. After the First World War there was a fashion, particularly in large town churches, to erect a screen often of rather lumpish proportions, as a war memorial. How much better it would have been to emulate Robert Bakewell. He got it absolutely right; nothing impinges, no-one is excluded, liturgically you can see and be seen, and aesthetically this screen is a most beautiful adornment, the crowning feature of the church.

❀ THE PAVILION, WREST PARK

Bedfordshire   OS 153 093347

The old house at Wrest Park, three-quarters of a mile east of Silsoe near Ampthill, mainly Tudor but with a late seventeenth-century front, was demolished in the 1830s. In its place the second Earl de Grey whose family had held the estate for over five hundred years and who was the first president of the (then merely) Institute of British Architects, built his château; and château it is, for he turned, somewhat surprisingly to a little-known French architect, Cléphane, who designed him something very French indeed. It is quite good, but wrong for Bedfordshire. However, it is not the house (nor the Orangery by the same architect) that you go to Wrest to see; it is the gardens.

The great garden is the creation of the earl's ancestor, the Duke of Kent, who between 1706 and 1740 had them laid out in the semi-formal manner then fashionable and made famous by Bridgeman, with water in every direction to attract the eye, rides, alleys, vistas, ornaments, statues and conceits. They were later altered by Capability Brown who with less formality surrounded the house on three sides with a serpentine stream and opened up the garden. There is plenty to see; pleasant parterres, a 'rustic ruin' beside a cascade bridge, attributed by Horace Walpole, a visitor here, to Brown himself, and a 'Chinese' bridge of 1874. Nothing is especially exciting, but all most agreeable.

It is true that the gardens suffer somewhat from being nearly all flat. Moreover, the site of the later house was moved back three hundred yards or more north from the Long Water, the great feature of the Duke's design, and artistically this was surely a mistake. It leaves something of a hiatus between the new house and the canal, an uneasy gap filled only with partial success by the Marble Fountain in the middle of the French garden. Here there are some good lead statues perhaps by Carpentière, and lead turns up again in his statue of William III at the other end of the canal, and in some eighteenth-century urns which flank the Bowling Green

House. This lies to the south-west; it is Palladian in style, of about 1740, and is attributed to Batty Langley the architectural writer and author of the well-known pattern books.

What undoubtedly gives the most pleasure is the straight stretch of water, known as the Long Water, with a basin at its northern (house) end and the symmetrical placing of the Pavilion six hundred yards or more away to the south. The architect is Thomas Archer and the date 1709–11. It is a delight and looks particularly well from a distance. Near to it appears quite a sizeable building, of red and yellow brick, which may at one time have been subjected to stucco. Only the doorway, which faces north towards the house is stone, and most original and excellent it is. The main apartment is a circular saloon, spacious and lofty, with a dome and lantern above. It has three rectangular and three semi-circular recesses, and these are all adorned in *trompè l'oeil* – simulated architecture all painted on a grey-blue ground. Two separate and narrow staircases lead to tiny servants' rooms above.

Thomas Archer was well-educated and much travelled, and the European baroque influence of Austria, Germany and Italy show more often in his buildings perhaps than in those of his English contemporaries. He was moreover a gentleman architect, an amateur in that as a man of means he did not have to rely on architectural commissions for a living. Nevertheless he worked successfully and competently on a number of houses for the aristocracy (at Chatsworth, for example and at Cliveden) and has three complete churches to his name, including St. John, Smith Square, in Westminster.* His pavilion at Wrest shows marked personality; it is certainly the right building in the right place.

*A memorial of the life and work of Alec Clifton-Taylor was held in this church on 1 July 1985.

THE WEST MIDLANDS

GLOUCESTERSHIRE HEREFORDSHIRE SHROPSHIRE STAFFORDSHIRE WARWICKSHIRE

Previous page: Sezincote

❦ ST. MARY & ST. DAVID, KILPECK

Herefordshire

Herefordshire is strong in Norman survivals: fonts, tympana, even complete churches, and Kilpeck about six miles south-west of Hereford, is the most perfect romanesque village church in England. It was begun probably about 1134 and owes its preservation to the most durable of the Old Red Sandstones. Naturally enough the church is by no means unrestored – Cottingham did a good job in 1848 – but the glorious corbel-table running all round the church just under the eaves is mainly original and alive with some of the most entertaining sculptures of the entire Middle Ages. It has, in the words of Nikolaus Pevsner, 'an irresistible comic-strip character'. It has a wealth of sculptural detail; pagan and Christian subjects jostle each other, bubbling with vitality; they are remarkably expressive, and a riot of fancy. This is a distinctly rustic church, and the appeal of the rubble-stone walls depends primarily on a rough peasant texture and the colour, a mixture of pink, buff and grey.

A more mature hand appears to have been at work on the doorway, the only one, to the south, protected for a long time by a porch. The work is masterly. The outer jambs of the door show coiled serpents, hideous and fat, biting each other's tails – a Viking influence, rare in England. In the shafts, at the west window, in the gable, a stylistic connection with Shobdon (p. 233) has been observed. Those at the door are surprising: among scrolled foliage two long thin wiry warriors sporting peaked hats and wearing tight-fitting trousers appear. The capital above has a lion and fantastic monster with a coiled tail. It is difficult to believe that all this sculpture is over eight hundred years old; if it had any symbolical meaning, it is no longer apparent and matters not at all. It is the sheer vitality and imagination that count; and no-one in the twelfth century would have called the creators of these astounding works sculptors. They were just stone-masons assigned to carving. Kilpeck no doubt owed its adornment to the presence of a Benedictine Priory close by; lucky for Kilpeck, and lucky for us, for this church is a precious survivor.

St. Mary & St. David,
Kilpeck

STOKESAY CASTLE GATEHOUSE

Stokesay Castle, in the Welsh Marshes, eight miles north-west of Ludlow, is justly famous as one of the earliest stone fortified houses, and is built in the hard local Silurian limestone. By 1291 Laurence de Ludlow, an up-and-coming lawyer with some social pretension, had given it curtain walls, a tower and a moat, now alas dry. However this house, very likeable and well-kept, was not built to be defended since the militant Welsh had already been tamed by Edward I. Stokesay was converted to a castle, because then, as now, a castle was a good address. It was last inhabited in 1727.

The half-timbered gatehouse, a delightful addition dating from the last thirty years of the sixteenth century, should be better appreciated. It is a gem. It stands on a stone floor as does the gatehouse at King's Pyon (p.224), although it is a much grander affair altogether. There are lozenges in the gable and diamonds at the first storey, and pilasters in the doorway. The infill is a lovely yellow ochre off-setting the oak, a little too dark perhaps, but not excessively so. It is thankfully 'unblacked', and so the wood is left largely in a natural state to speak for itself, and that is how this wonderful material should always be treated. At the brackets and corner-posts there is some fine carving, endearing objects of fantasy amid a real touch of the Renaissance. What fun those craftsmen had!

ST. MARY (FORMERLY DORE ABBEY), ABBEY DORE

Herefordshire   *OS 149 387304*

St. Mary, Abbey Dore, set in the Golden Valley, thirteen miles south-west of Hereford (about five from Kilpeck), occupies what was once the eastern part of a large Cistercian abbey church. It is mainly Early English, dating from about 1175 to 1220, and built of red sandstone with grey limestone dressings. After the Dissolution the abbey became ruinous, and what is left is a fragment, sizeable enough without a doubt for a parish church, and restored in about 1633 by Lord Scudamore. It was he who added the tower above the first bay of the ambulatory at the south-east corner of the crossing. From the outside the Abbey looks strangely eccentric and brooding, as if still suffering the ravages of the Dissolution.

The interior tells a very different story, and to step inside is to experience a positive shock of pleasure. The design is of singular richness and purity, and the beautiful shafting at the arches is immediately apparent. Lovely cross-vistas, too, emerge, and behind the high altar the ambulatory ends in a marvellous double walk, its roof carried by four lofty slender piers, again with delightful shafts. There is plenty of stiff-leaf too at the capitals, with delicate carved detail. There are also some beautiful early fourteenth-century bosses lying about, not *in situ*, which means of course they can be appreciated at really close quarters. Lord Scudamore's oak screen presents something of a problem. It has somewhat clumsy columns, balusters between, and a heavy cornice surmounted by obelisks and a coat of arms. It makes a strong impression; indeed a little too strong for some tastes. Not enough, however, to detract from the beauty of the choir beyond.

There are alas blemishes. In 1932, an incumbent was buried in an ugly white marble tomb, with a kerb, in the nave of all places, quite close to the door. What an appalling example to set to his parishioners!

❦ THE LEY, WEOBLEY

Herefordshire   OS *149 392512*

Opposite:
The Ley, Weobley

*C*ider, cattle, Old Red Sandstone and timber-frame; this is Herefordshire, one of England's most unspoiled counties. Above all timber-frame, which until the industrial revolution was the normal construction for vernacular buildings throughout virtually the whole county. At Weobley, twelve miles north-west of Hereford, it is to be seen in profusion, especially in Broad Street, just behind the Red Lion with its famous and much photographed cruck-framed house. Three-quarters of a mile to the south-west, at the end of a lane which seems to lead nowhere, is a much grander affair, the Ley (pronounced 'lay') with its principal front facing north-north-west.

It is a fine sight, a lovely house in a most attractive silvery oak; how much better than the still all too frequent black and white to be seen all over England! Nearly all of its windows are very suitably glazed with diamond panes and over the door is a coat of arms and the date 1589. The great pleasure of this house is in the gables – seven in all in jolly array: two at the wings, one at the centre, one at the arch set off to the right, and three for the bay windows. The rectangle of the frames shows a welcome and almost dignified reticence after some of the jazzy patterns of the West Midlands. The gable over the bay window at the middle has some pargetting – a plaster sun, a spray of thistles and some oak leaves – decorative work unusual for Herefordshire and more often at home in East Anglia. Under the gables at the top there are some fancy diamond patterns carved in the wood.

The Ley is a real joy; the quintessence of traditional English building at its most lovely. It is surrounded by fertile fields and it is in reality a farm house, albeit one in the top rank. What a fortunate farmer.

❦ ST. JAMES, and THE MARKET HALL CHIPPING CAMPDEN

Gloucestershire   *St. James OS 151 155395*
                                           Market Hall OS 151 152392

*T*he market-town of Campden (for Chipping or chepying means 'market') in Gloucestershire has scarcely one false note from end to end; if Cotswold people are somewhat smug about their surroundings they have every reason to be, for theirs are the showpieces of England. Chipping Campden is packed full of delights, all built in a beautiful golden oolite from Westington quarry just a mile up the hill, which gives the town quality, dignity and a great uniformity. We must confine ourselves to two of the town's pleasures; the Market Hall, and the church, and more especially the tower, built, like so many other marvels of the Perpendicular throughout the county, 'on the backs of sheep'. For Campden was, from the thirteenth

to the seventeenth century, an important centre for wool, England's chief export, and had a weekly market as early as 1247.

The church tower is best seen from the south-east, and the model was the cathedral at Gloucester, as Wells was for Somerset. It is splendidly proportioned, with a glorious parapet, and the masoncraft is beyond praise. The date is mid-fifteenth century. It is a typically Gloucestershire creation, but with one unusual detail – the manner in which subsidiary pinnacles spring from ogee arches in front of the parapet. Perhaps it is more curious here than beautiful, but in every other respect this is a stylish stately tower, beautifully sited, the hallmark of the town.

The Market Hall stands detached in the High Street, and is now in the excellent care of the National Trust. It was not, it appears, connected with the wool trade, but was intended for the sale of cheese, butter and poultry. For a small building it is well endowed with no fewer than ten gables all beautifully roofed in Stonesfield stone slates, and it has five by two bays providing an open arcade with a stone balustrade. It has an interesting and complicated roof, exposed from underneath and shows the slates, fixed to their battens. The floor is paved with large stone blocks. It was erected in 1627 by Sir Baptist Hicks, Lord Campden, a great benefactor of the town and church, and his coat of arms appears at one end under an ogee gable. He lies buried in the church in the large family chapel south of the chancel and is commemorated in a notable monument, sumptuous in execution if wrong in colour and material for it is of black and white marble.

Chipping Campden, with all its pleasures is in a class of its own; it is perhaps the most enjoyable of all the small towns in England.

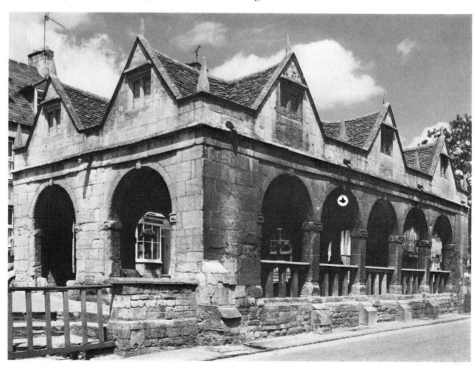

Chipping Campden:
right: Market Hall
far right: St. James

216

'Wynyates,' said the guide, 'is probably a corruption of "Windygates" or "Vineyards".' Be that as it may, the former mediaeval vineyards provide the backdrop to this most exquisite of houses,* a heavenly sight in an enchanting setting right in the centre of a tree-girt basin, surrounded by gardens. It is built of a great variety of materials; soft rose-red brick,** partly Tudor, partly Georgian, predominates in a whole range of colour from orange to brown and umber black; then there are dressings in a grey-yellowish limestone, and a lovely lichened grey stone roof with very small stone slates, almost certainly from Stonesfield, about fourteen miles away. There is oak, too, for the half-timbering of the two gables on the south-west entrance front, and these are one of the few weaknesses of the house, for they are too dark in tone and 'jump out', because, no doubt for the purposes of preservation, the beams have been coated with a creosote which has left them nearly black.

In essence the house is still much as it was, built by Sir William Compton in the sixteenth century. It is a courtyard house, originally with a wide moat which was filled in by order of the Cromwellians in about 1650. Part of it in the 1950s was dug

out again and filled with water on the north-west side of the house. The courtyard is small, and not stylish, but has a kind of intimate charm. The brick here is mainly Tudor, hand made of course, with blue diapers, but at the top, almost all round, it is Georgian, and the divide is clearly visible. The lead rainwater heads, some even boasting Corinthian capitals, are dated 1732, and the twisted moulded chimneys testify to the newly discovered luxury of the Tudor fire-place.

The north-east side of the house dates from 1730 but this is only an outer face. New rooms were built up against existing ones which meant blocking up windows along the north-east side of the hall. The windows throughout are quite a puzzle and vary in date from the sixteenth to the nineteenth century. Some blocking is explained by the sorry tale of the owner, the Earl of Northampton, who, in 1768, went bankrupt through gambling and fighting a recklessly extravagant Parliamentary election in Northampton. His order to pull the house down came from Switzerland; but the agent did not obey; he met the debts by avoiding the tax on the windows by blocking them, and disposing by sale of the contents.

The Big Hall, within, on the collegiate pattern of screen, gallery and dais is largely reconstructed. In the Dining-Room there is an elegant plaster ceiling, said to date from about 1620, which if this is true, is very good for its florid period, but the best room is the Drawing Room, rather lovely of its kind, with another plaster ceiling reputedly Elizabethan, and a fireplace and panelling undoubtedly so, brought from Canonbury House, Islington, in about 1860. In the chapel, detached to the north of the house, nearly everything is modern, including a good window by Sir Ninian Comper, 1930, modelled on the Tudor one destroyed in 1644, and most appropriate.

During the 1939–45 war, Compton Wynyates gave valuable service to the nation as a store for treasures from the British Museum. Sadly after a number of years in which it was opened regularly, Compton Wynyates is difficult to visit as the owner now lives there permanently. It is greatly to be hoped that on occasion it will be possible for the public to see again this delightful building in its wonderful scenic setting; for it is the English dream house.

*'The most perfect in England in the specific picturesque, completely irregular mode' – Nikolaus Pevsner, *The Buildings of England: Warwickshire*.
**'Probably made *in situ*; remains of open brick kilns were found near the long pond.' – Douglas Hickman, *Warwickshire* a Shell Guide.

❀ PITCHFORD HALL

Shropshire   OS 126 527043

Because of its comparative lack of good building stone, the West Midlands, more than any other region of England – even East Anglia – is regarded as the home of timber-frame, and indeed of 'black-and-white'. Quite when 'black-and-white' became the fashion is difficult to determine. It appears that some timber buildings were painted, albeit lightly with water-paint, quite early on in the Elizabethan and Jacobean period; but the hard permanent black, a product of tar and pitch distilled from coal, only became available in the nineteenth century. Then it became universally taken up, no doubt with the best but misguided intentions of preserving the wood, but also because it was felt to look smart. It became a fashion that bounced all round the country; not only on decent mediaeval buildings that had done nothing to deserve it, but also as a sham, in the form of paint on plaster in the gables to look like wood. Nowadays there is a quite correct preference to 'de-black', for a material as sturdy as oak needs no such drastic treatment. We should be deeply grateful.

Timber-frame comes in all shapes and sizes and conditions, and Pitchford Hall is very large and black-and-white. It lies about seven and a half miles south-east of Shrewsbury and was built in about 1560–70 on an E-plan. Originally the entrance was to the north which is now the garden. So the house, set in fine parkland and approached by a grand avenue of limes, now faces south, with kitchen and dining-room to the west, and great chamber and drawing room to the east. At first floor, on the entrance side a long corridor runs the length of the house. The interior is heavily panelled and the woodwork looks much renewed, although in the drawing room, which has a pleasant plaster ceiling and a delightful bow window overlooking a stream, there is what resembles good seventeenth-century work with fluted pilasters.

Pitchford Hall was built on the site of a mediaeval manor house, and stands on red sandstone foundations. Outside the diagonal strut is the overwhelming and favourite motif, the lozenge within lozenge; these are the familiar diamond shapes that used sometimes to turn up as a remedy for sore throats. There is not much decorative work except at the base of the gables on the east side, and at the porch which has a somewhat fanciful upper storey above a carved bressummer. There are wavy supports with quatrefoils to left and right of a large diamond-shaped eighteenth-century clock, a little heavy perhaps, but handsomely painted on a blue ground. Above, the turret ends in a stepped jaunty ogee with finial. The windows have rectangular leaded lights, all present and correct, but unfortunately the timbers were painted a dark *café au lait* about fifty years ago and traces of this are still to be seen.

The chief pleasures of Pitchford Hall, however, are at the roof where the sandstone slates are wonderful. All the original slates were taken off some thirty years ago while the timbers were restored and then put back. Care has to be taken to keep the roof well ventilated since sandstone is attractive to lichen and other fungi which will rot the timbers again, but this roof with its delightful swept valleys at the points of junction now looks magnificent and a real embellishment to the house. The brick chimney-stacks are grouped together on the ridges of the roof; they may be restored but they are robust and confident and quite theatrical in feeling.

Shropshire* has a lot of black-and-white to show but nothing to compare with Pitchford Hall. Because of its setting amongst the trees and the park, and because of its oak and stone, so right in this locality, it is not only grand, but in every way it feels at home.

*Nikolaus Pevsner's *The Buildings of England: Shropshire*, 1958, has the dedication 'For Alec after twenty-five years'. In all the later volumes, Alec Clifton-Taylor contributed separate sections to the Introduction on building materials. His last, in the revised volume on Devon, will be published in 1987.

Overleaf:
Pitchford Hall

221

HONINGTON HALL

Gatepiers topped by pineapples, a five-arched classical bridge across the Warwickshire Stour and a sweeping drive announce the arrival at Honington, a perfect example of the late seventeenth-century house. The date is 1682. The entrance front faces east, and now, particularly since the later addition to the north has been demolished, it displays a most perfect symmetry, disturbed only on a warm day by windows understandably left open but which jazz up the effect of the glazing bars.

For this house is correct in almost every respect; it has fine brickwork, now happily relieved of its creeper, beautifully offset by brown stone dressings surely from the same Hornton quarry that yielded the stone for Broughton Castle across the border in Oxfordshire. There is also a delightful cornice and a lovely hipped roof complete with dormers and hand made tiles. The doorway is flanked by Corinthian

Opposite:
Pitchford Hall

Below:
Honington Hall

columns surmounted by the flourish of a coat of arms, and in the oval recesses above the ground-floor windows are busts of emperors. On the north side of the house another doorway has an enchanting hood decorated with flowers and leaves, and a cherub's head. Across the courtyard the stables, of seventeenth-century date, are complemented by an octagonal dovecot. Rusticated and segmented gateways lead to the garden, and beyond, to the south, is a veranda with Tuscan columns.

Within are a glorious entrance hall (added about 1744), sumptuous plasterwork, a riot of Rococo with thick garlands, and an octagonal saloon, in the style of Kent, with a fine coffered dome. Honington Hall is a beautiful house, beautifully kept.

Honington Hall:
door hood

❦ *BUTTHOUSE GATEHOUSE, KING'S PYON*

Herefordshire *OS 149 436502*

There are a number of timber-framed lodges in the West Midlands, which echo in miniature the large house for which they stand sentinel, and one such, the gatehouse for the Butthouse, at King's Pyon, is a delight. It is built on a plinth of the local sandstone, with a projecting, or oversailing, upper storey on all sides, and is dated 1632. The bressummer, the main beam which supports the superstructure, is carved in the customary way, with dragons and scrolls, and so are the barge-boards which form the apex of the gables, beautifully clad throughout with hand made tiles. It is more like a dolls' house than a gatehouse and might be thought somewhat cramped for modern living! It may be a miniature, but what a joy it is!

Opposite:
Butthouse Gatehouse

Stanway, four miles north-east of Winchcombe, is situated directly on the limestone belt. Moreover it is the oolitic limestone, the best (and the most expensive) of all the limestones since it has a sufficiently fine grain to yield a freestone or ashlar; that is stone which could be cut 'freely' and fashioned in any direction with mallet, saw or chisel. There was not only plenty of stone in this area, but it was easy to work; it could be prised from the quarry in huge blocks, sometimes as much as five feet square, and it was soft enough when first cut to be worked to provide refinements and embellishments in plenty for buildings which give the Cotswolds such pride of place in the pattern of English building. Stanway, like many other villages in the Cotswolds, had its own quarry – the Jackdaw Quarry just up the hill. Quarries were everywhere, some of them famous, yielding a celebrated ashlar; in Gloucestershire alone there was Painswick, Chipping Campden,

Mitcheldean, Slaughter, Cirencester, Little Barrington, and Temple Guiting which provided the stone for the house and gatehouse at Stanway.

The house was built between 1580 and 1640 on the site of the manor which had for eight centuries belonged to the Abbey of Tewkesbury before it came into the ownership of the Tracy family. Parts of the earlier buildings were incorporated into the new house and there were to be alterations in the eighteenth and nineteenth centuries; the west entrance front looks Victorian and not very good at that, and in this present century there was another alteration by Detmar Blow which only lasted thirty-five years. The roofs are all of stone and lovely, and especially delightful and perhaps unique in the cresting on the south front. Otherwise the only decoration is at the doorways, and the overall appearance while not lacking in charm is therefore somewhat sober-sided. The unbroken ranges of windows, mullioned and transomed, are also rather bleak; in short this house is under-ornamented and over-fenestrated.

The gatehouse too is something of an oddity, but decidedly picturesque. To the south, as you enter, it is a little grandiose, of three storeys and with a Tudor arch flanked by fluted columns with the Tracy arms above and scallops to either side and three gables surmounted by more shells. The interior elevation is quite different, for the arch here has pedimented doorways each side (giving access to what is a pair of lodges) but with oval windows and an oriel above. More shells appear again, a decidedly fishy concoction! This then is a mixture of the classical and Gothic; both sides are in fact bastards.

It is the excellent stone, however, which lends both these buildings such distinction; this is the orange yellow of Guiting but with quite a lot of grey lichen so that the orange is less emphatic, which is all to the good. The architect is unknown, although David Verey* has suggested Timothy Strong or his son Valentine, the founders of an extraordinary family business of master masons who worked to the designs of Wren and Hawksmoor, and whose fortunes were based on the ownership of the quarries at Little Barrington in Gloucestershire and Taynton in Oxfordshire. They worked on the Canterbury Quad at St. John's College, Oxford, and Valentine was also concerned with the building of two Gloucestershire manor houses at Lower Slaughter and Fairford.

There are also at Stanway a vast garden wall, contemporary with the Tudor house, an eye-catcher of a Vanbrughian pyramid to the east, the church, with a lively twelfth-century corbel-table and pleasant small Perpendicular tower, and a magnificent tithe barn. This was built in the fourteenth century for the Abbot of Tewkesbury, and it has a superb roof, arch-braced with collars, and tremendously robust timbers which come half-way down the walls. These walls are solid stone, four feet thick, but it is a pity that the lower part of the walls inside has had to suffer the indignity of cement facing.

No one building at Stanway merits unqualified admiration, but the group gives great pleasure. It is a lovely sequence of buildings; the secret is the stone; there is not a stranger amongst them, and they all belong.

*The Buildings of England: Gloucestershire: the Cotswolds, David Verey, Penguin, reprinted 1974.

✤ ST. MARY, INGESTRE

Staffordshire

Thereere can be no greater contrast at Ingestre four miles east-north-east of Stafford than that between the church and the house; brash brick at the Hall, refined ashlar at the church. The stone is a sandstone, and looks as if it came, certainly at least for the restoration, from Hollington, near Uttoxeter. It is predominantly pinkish in colour and so soft in the quarry that it can be brought out in large blocks, and cut like cheese. With exposure to the air it becomes much harder and has had a successful role in some important modern building and restoration, for example at Coventry Cathedral, Hereford Cathedral and the parish church at Ludlow.

Left and overleaf:
St. Mary, Ingestre

*St. Mary
Ingestre:
nave.
Far right,
ceiling
plasterwork*

The church at Ingestre has something of the air of a private chapel, although it is the parish church. It is dated 1676, and almost everybody, although there is no conclusive documentary proof, thinks in architectural terms of Wren; he was a friend of Walter Chetwynd, owner of the Hall at that time and like him a member of the Royal Society, and he produced a drawing of 'Mr. Chetwynd's Tower'. Without and within the marvellous quality of the design lends further support to the attribution. The tower, almost exactly twice the height of the nave, rises over a pedimented doorway and is in admirable keeping with the proportions of the rest of the church. There are garlands and shields at the pediment, and garlands again around the clock, and a pleasant balustrade capped at each corner with urns. An inscription over the porch reads 'Deo Optimo Maximo', and the whole church bears witness to that theme.

This is a sumptuous interior, rich, vigorous, and almost unaltered, and how greatly it benefits from having no galleries to intrude upon this wonderful feeling of unity. The screen, in three parts with pilasters, uncluttered by too much detail and with the royal arms above is of the highest quality, and the panelling in the chancel and the pulpit with its tester (is it a little top-heavy?) are worthy companions. The *pièce de résistance* is the ceiling, clearly separated into compartments as was the last Stuart fashion; flat and gloriously decorated above the nave, coved and somewhat less elaborate over the chancel. It is exquisite, and almost unbelievable in a small parish church, bearing comparison with many more ambitious works in houses and churches of a similar date.

The blemishes are minor; the stained glass is really rather indifferent, particularly the Morris window in the north aisle, and the font, with its bulbous stem is by no means a happy example of the style of Charles II. The monuments to Chetwynds and Talbots and a hyphenated mixture of the two are overbearing; none is aesthetically satisfying and they are too all-pervasive. By any modest count there are at least ten, and one in black marble with shining bronze is quite out of place here. They are altogether *de trop*. The light fittings, made of wrought iron, were installed in 1886. They are delicate and not at all unwelcome, but perhaps more a curiosity than a work of art.

St. Mary, Ingestre is a lovely church; it is without a doubt the most distinguished country church of the late Stuart period in England.

ST. JOHN EVANGELIST, SHOBDON

Herefordshire

Herefordshire is perhaps, because it is still so extremely rural, England's most beautiful county. In its north-west corner, eight miles west of Leominster, only four miles from the Welsh border with Radnorshire (now wretchedly renamed Powys), it harbours a delightful *vaut le voyage* for the amateur of churches.

St. John Evangelist, Shobdon, lies about three-quarters of a mile remote from the village to the north; it was in mediaeval days the church of a priory which housed the famous Herefordshire workshop of Norman sculpture* whose master-mason was later to work at Kilpeck. In the seventeenth century it became virtually the exclusive property of the Bateman family whose country seat occupied the site of the former monastery. Be prepared for a surprise, made all the more exciting by the approach, best on foot, along a track from the village.

At first appearances there is nothing special, a thirteenth-century tower, broad, somewhat short and unbuttressed, a small castellated church set amongst forest trees and clipped yew. The masonry, a little rougher on the tower than elsewhere, is excellent; a grey-buff sandstone, perfectly in tune with the surroundings. But look at the windows, and especially the door at the base of the tower. Here is the tell-tale ogee, and within we find a fantastic, a unique interior. This is the result of an almost complete rebuilding of the mediaeval church undertaken by John, the second Lord Bateman, much influenced by his uncle, Richard, a friend of Horace Walpole, who, following the example of Strawberry Hill (1751) had embraced Gothick. Horace Walpole, Sir Nikolaus Pevsner tells us, converted Lord Bateman 'from a Chinese to a Goth' (i.e. from the taste for chinoiserie to Gothick). It certainly seems to have been a conversion of some ardour for the church is now transformed: 'an enchanting toy-theatre interpretation of a mediaeval interior' as Graham Hutton† has so rightly perceived.

Below, and right: St. John Evangelist, Shobdon: interior

The reworking‡ of the interior dates from 1752–6, and in 1963 it was beautifully

repaired and faithfully restored by the Historic Churches Preservation Trust. What most impresses is the unity of the whole, all decked out in a most pleasing livery, white and pale blue. The ceiling is coved and decorated, stucco everywhere and Gothick panels between the windows. The transepts and chancel are separated by tripartite arches, rich in ogee, pendant and ornament, and at the west end is a gallery. This houses the organ, which if you have to have one, seems absolutely right here. It is correct in scale, tastefully designed, and inconspicuously sited so as neither to interfere with the perspective of the nave nor the symmetry of the chancel.

There are a pulpit, reading-desk, and clerk's stall, the fashionable Georgian three-decker, all very much designed as a piece with the rest of the church. The pulpit has an elaborate tester and is adorned with crimson velvet hangings. By comparison the desk is a little clumsy, as perhaps are also the pews with rather over-large bench ends and heavy quatrefoils above the ogee motif. Nonetheless, they are impeccable Gothick and all painted as part of the colour scheme.

The south transept houses the Bateman family pew, fitted out with comfortable chairs as a protection against interminable sermonising, and during the rigours of the winter, a fire would be provided in the large Gothick fireplace. The railings are boarded against draughts. No such comforts attended the servants' pew in the north; the writ of the country house ran here too in these drawing-rooms of the Lord!

The charm of this amusing interior has, alas, two jarring notes. The east window of 1907, wisely unsigned, is dreadfully inappropriate, a poor design of ghastly colour which serves only to blot out the light. It is a memorial to the second Lord Bateman but since the title has been extinct for fifty years, this window too should surely be extinguished. The other 'intruder', though far less conspicuous, is the Norman font, a likeable bumpkin, with four primitive lions round the stem, but not specially good, and decidedly *de trop* here, for Shobdon has its own Gothick version. The Norman font came from the twelfth-century church and was removed in 1756 to do long service as a garden ornament, an interesting comment on eighteenth-century ideas of mediaeval art and the picturesque. It should not have been returned; it is ill at ease here and would best be offered as a gift to another Norman church in Herefordshire which has not one of its own. Shobdon church is an essay in Gothick, entire to itself.

*Fragments of this sculpture which survived the rebuilding of the church are now incorporated at Shobdon Arches, a folly erected in the park of Shobdon Court just north of the church.

†*English Parish Churches:* Edwin Smith, Olive Cook and Graham Hutton, Thames and Hudson, 1976, p. 167.

‡The architect is unknown. H.M. Colvin does not confirm Flitcroft (Pevsner, *The Buildings of England: Herefordshire*, p. 288) although he had worked at Shobdon Court, Lord Bateman's seat close by, in 1746. 'What seems certain', Mr. Colvin explains, 'is that the architect was not the local Gothicist Pritchard whom Bateman sacked.' Thereafter he presumably turned to the metropolitan taste, though there is no authority to determine who was responsible.

St. John Evangelist, Shobdon: pulpit

❧ SEZINCOTE

Gloucestershire *OS 151 172312*

'**A** good joke, but a good house too' recorded D. Talbot Rice about Sezincote (pronounced 'Seize-in-coat') and the comment is not far from the mark. The house lies near the northern limits of Gloucestershire, and almost equidistant from the county boundaries with Worcestershire, Warwickshire and Oxfordshire. It stands in a large and lovely park, and although beautifully sited with a fine view, it faces east. In essence it is a late-Georgian house with perfectly normal sash windows with glazing bars on the upper floor, although the lower-floor windows still unfortunately have Victorian plate glass. The Georgian house, which is purely classical Greek revival, has been encased in a skin, oriental and undeniably exotic for England, and this adds a delightful dimension to the repertoire of the English country house.

Sezincote (the name is derived from 'Cheine-cote, that is hillside of the oaks', from the French 'chêne' and the old English 'cote'), was designed by the architect Samuel Pepys Cockerell, brother of Sir Charles who began to remodel an existing house in 1805. Samuel had already designed nearby Daylesford for Warren Hastings and provided there a Moslem dome; Indian motifs were also to be the dominating influence at Sezincote, for Sir Charles himself had made a fortune in the East India Company before returning to the life of an English country gentleman. At Sezincote the architect had the help of Thomas Daniell, the Indian topographical artist, whose work is seen to great advantage in the Victoria Museum in Calcutta. He was better versed in Indian architecture than any other European of his day and to him must surely be attributed the detail of the Hindu motifs around the doors and windows. Moslem influence too is evident at the fanciful yet graceful onion-shaped dome, the *chattris*, the umbrella-like minarets at the corners of the roof and the very deep *chujja* which projects at eaves level. The dome and the chimneys are of copper, the usual copper verdigris, a veridian green, and most successful. The principal material, however, is a local yellow-orange limestone, said to have been artificially stained to give it a more correct Indian hue. The decorative panelling to the outside of the house (especially on the south and east) is most refined and charming and in the best tradition of the Cotswold masons. Because their work is in such good stone nothing looks gimcrack, but the overall mélange (unless you have seen Lutyens at work in New Delhi) does at first appear a little odd.

Away to the south-west stretches a curving orangery, mostly glass and extremely pretty, and behind it the wooded hill provides a steep and effective background. It was originally intended to have a similar balancing addition to the north-west but only the little end pavilion was erected: the 'tent' room imitated at the Brighton Pavilion in 1815, and hung within with silk on poles. The orangery was restored from a near-derelict state in the 1950s in a synthetic Cotswold stone, somewhat whitish, and cast to patterns taken from a mould – a perfectly proper and successful solution. It had to be repaired in 1980!

Beyond the entrance hall is the staircase, under the dome, but the latter is not visible from below. The staircase starts in two flights of stairs which meet and then goes up in a sloping bridge carried on ornamental iron girders, making a remarkably good effect. At the top of the bridge it divides again under a ceiling scalloped at the corner – altogether a most original and elegant feature. The grand reception rooms are all at first-floor level, and it is here that the main architectural interest lies; the Saloon, more Regency than Georgian (the Prince Regent was a visitor here, probably in 1806) has a lofty coved ceiling, and window hangings looped in festoons. The main bedroom (over the Drawing Room), has a segmented ceiling somewhat à la Soane, a beautiful marble fireplace and an overall elegance. The most westerly of the bedrooms on the southern front has a hilarious four-poster in the spirit of the house, and a remarkable recent *trompe l'oeil* painting (c. 1964) by Geoffrey Ghing.

Humphrey Repton was consulted about the garden (as indeed he was about the house) which runs down the hill to the north-east. Water is the great asset in this layout. In the distance is a lake, long and narrow with attractive views back to the house, and pools, dropping in steps, one presided over by a goddess. It is not hard to see Thomas Daniell's hand again at work. It was he who made designs for the Indian bridge, an exotic temple in effect, which carries the drive over a delightfully landscaped little valley. Tranquil and rather lush, the gardens make the perfect foil for Sezincote, a most original and unusual house and, without doubt, a building of true delight.

ENVOI

What have all these Buildings of Delight in common? They are all, first and foremost, buildings which give pleasure, and it is not without significance, nor indeed regret, that there is no building included in these pages later than 1877. It was a continual sadness to Alec Clifton-Taylor to find himself, in architecture, so out of sympathy with our times. The causes he identified as largely economic; many architects would be delighted to build with the traditional materials especially stone, which was his great love, if it were financially possible to do so. What feature here then are buildings made of timber and plaster, handmade brick and tile, and above all stone. The craftsmen too, working in wood, plaster and iron, play a prominent part. These are buildings which are invariably built of materials obtained locally; so they look right, they pay respect to the spirit of place, they are human in scale, and live happily with their neighbours. Nowhere here will you find high-rise buildings or large slabs of exposed concrete, for though a fine material structurally it neither weathers nor grows mellow; nearly always it cracks, stains, and becomes shabby.

Alec Clifton-Taylor's original list from which this selection of a hundred buildings has been made numbered one hundred and sixty-six. The process of reduction has been heart-rending. It has in part been determined by the constraints involved in producing any book of this kind – the geographical spread of location and the need in a relatively short space of time to visit as many of the sites as possible – but also because some buildings had been altered or neglected to the point of almost being unrecognisable in the terms in which he described them only a few years ago. Others, of course, have been restored and rehabilitated with immeasurable benefit.

The moral is constant vigilance; Alec Clifton-Taylor, perhaps more than any other because of the breadth and success of his appeal, contributed enormously to the cause of sympathetic understanding and the need for sensible and proper conservation. He made us all much more keenly aware of our inheritance and opened our eyes to new ways of looking at our surroundings. He regarded that, together with giving pleasure to people, as his most important goal in life. How well he succeeded!

Alec Clifton-Taylor died on 1st April 1985. The closing words of his last television programme seem a fitting summary of his life and work. 'If you love architecture as I do,' he said as he boarded the train leaving Durham, 'you'll never come to the end of England.'

GLOSSARY

ABACUS: the flat slab on top of a capital on which the architrave rests.

AEDICULE: an opening – door, window, or niche – framed by columns and a pediment.

AMBULATORY: a processional aisle closing a sanctuary or an apse.

ANNULET: a ring round a pier or shaft.

APSE: a semi-circular or polygonal end to a church or chapel.

ARCADE: a range of arches resting on piers or columns; a 'blind arcade' is an arcade attached to a wall.

ARCHITRAVE: 1. The lowest of the three divisions of the Classical entablature, below the frieze and cornice. 2. The moulded frame surrounding a door or window.

ASHLAR: Masonry of hewn or sawn stone, in blocks which are usually large but often quite thin, carefully squared and finely jointed in level courses.

BALL-FLOWER: a globular ornament of three-petalled flowers enclosing small balls.

BALUSTER: a small pillar or column, supporting a rail or coping.

BARGE-BOARD: a barge is the overhanging edge of a roof up the slope of a gable and the board, usually decoratively carved, masks and protects the ends of the horizontal roof timbers.

BATTEN: a strip of wood, used for attaching slates and tiles to a roof or wall.

BATTLEMENT: an indented parapet, used on churches for decorative effect.

BAY: a division of a building, inside or outside, marked not by walls but units of vaulting, arches, roof compartments or windows.

BOND: an arrangement of stone or bricks whereby the vertical joints in one course do not coincide with those in the courses above or below. *See also* ENGLISH and FLEMISH BOND.

BOSS: an ornamental projection used to conceal the intersection of ribs in a vault, or beams in a wooden ceiling.

BRACE: an inclined timber, straight or curved, introduced usually at an angle, to strengthen others.

BRACKET: a projection designed as a support.

BRESSUMMER: a horizontal beam supporting a superstructure.

BUTTRESS: masonry, or brickwork, built against a wall to provide stability or to counteract the outward thrust of an arch or vault.

CABLE: a convex moulding resembling a cable or rope.

CANTILEVER: a structural member which projects beyond the line of the support.

CAPITAL: the top part of a column (or pilaster).

CARTOUCHE: a tablet set in an ornate frame or scroll.

CASEMENT: a window hinged on one side, opening outwards or inwards.

CASTELLATED: decorated like a castle with turrets and battlements.

CHAMFER: a flat splayed edge between two flat plain surfaces.

CHEVRON: a zigzag form of ornamentation.

CLADDING: thin slabs of stone or other material used externally as a covering to the structure of a building.

CLERESTORY: the upper part of the nave, choir and transepts, containing a series of windows.

CLUNCH: a cretaceous chalk stone, soft and easily worked, best suited to interiors.

COFFERED: sunk moulded panels on the underside of arches.

COLONNADE: a row of columns supporting an entablature.

COPING: the capping of a wall to give weather protection.

CORBEL: a block of stone or piece of brickwork projecting from a wall to support a floor, roof, vault, parapet or other feature.

CORINTHIAN: *see* ORDERS.

CORNICE: topmost part of an entablature, and also any moulded projection which crowns the part to which it is fixed.

COURSE: a continuous layer of stone or brick of uniform height.

CRENELLATE: to fortify a residence with battlements and parapet.

CROCKETS: ornaments, usually in the form of buds or curled leaves, placed on the sloping sides of spires, gables, canopies and pinnacles.

CRUCK: a section of a curved tree split so that the two sections, one placed in reverse, formed a rough arch.

DECORATED: English Gothic architecture (c. 1290–1360) characterised by tracery, at first geometric, then flowing.

DENTILS: small rectangular tooth-like blocks under a cornice.

DIAPER: an all-over pattern usually of lozenge, square or diamond shapes.

DOG-TOOTH: a repeating ornament of four raised tooth-like pieces, usually set in a hollow moulding.

DOLOMITIC: *see* MAGNESIAN LIMESTONE.

DORIC: *see* ORDERS.

DORMER: a window projecting vertically from a sloping roof.

DRESSING: refinements of worked and finished stones – e.g. architraves, keystones, quoins etc.

DRIPSTONE: a projecting moulding over the heads of doorways and windows to throw off rain.

EARLY ENGLISH: English Gothic architecture, broadly covering the thirteenth century.

EAVES: horizontal overhang of a roof beyond a wall.

EMBATTLE: furnish with battlements; *see also* CRENELLATE.

ENGLISH BOND: bricks laid in alternate courses of all headers, only the short end visible, and all stretchers, the long side visible.

ENTABLATURE: the assembly in classical orders of architrave, frieze and cornice, supported by columns.

FENESTRATION: the arrangement of windows in a building.

FILLET: a small member between mouldings.

FINIAL: the topmost feature, generally ornamental, of a gable, roof, pinnacle, or canopy.

FLEMISH BOND: the method of laying bricks with every course consisting of alternating headers and stretchers. – *see* ENGLISH BOND.

FLUSHWORK: the decorative use of flint in conjunction with dressed stone to form patterns, monograms, and inscriptions.

FLUTED: vertical grooves, regular and concave, on a column.

FOIL - (TRE- QUATRE, *et seq*): a three, four or more – lobed ornamental infilling for a circle or arch-head.

FREESTONE: stone of sufficiently fine grain to be cut 'freely', in any direction, with saw, mallet or chisel.

FRIEZE: part of the entablature between architrave and cornice.

GABLE: triangular portion of wall at the end of a ridge roof: a *Dutch gable* is curved and shaped and surmounted by a pediment; a *stepped gable* has stepped sides.

GARGOYLE: a carved grotesque human or animal head serving as a spout from the top of a wall to throw off rainwater.

GAUGED BRICKWORK: the use of soft bricks rubbed to a precise dimension, very accurately laid and finely jointed; often used in dressings.

GEOMETRIC TRACERY: tracery of simple geometric shapes e.g. circles and trefoils.

GLAZING BARS: strips of wood enclosing panes of glass in a window.

GLORIETTE: a decorated chamber in a castle or other building.

GOTHIC: style of architecture in England spanning the 13th to 15th centuries; divided chronologically into Early English, Decorated, and Perpendicular.

GOTHICK: the recreation and re-interpretation of English Gothic architecture in the 18th century.

HAMMERBEAM: beams projecting at right angles from a wall, to provide support for the vertical members and/or arched braces of a wooden roof.

HERRINGBONE: the setting of stones, bricks or tiles, obliquely in alternate rows so as to form a zigzag pattern.

HIPPED ROOF: a pitched roof with sloped ends instead of vertical gables.

INTERSTICE: a narrow opening, chink or crevice.

IONIC: *see* ORDERS.

JAMB: the vertical side of an archway, doorway or window.

JESSE WINDOW: window in which glass or stonework forms a Tree of Jesse representing the lineage of Christ.

JETTY: the overhang of an upper floor on a timber-framed building.

KEEP: the massive inner tower or stronghold of a castle.

KEYSTONE: the central stone of an arch or ribbed vault.

KNAPPED FLINT: flint cobbles or nodules split across and used in walls with the split face showing.

LANCET: a narrow window terminating in a sharp point.

LANTERN: a small circular or polygonal turret with windows all round, crowning a roof or dome.

LATH: a thin, narrow, flat strip of wood, riven or sawn, used to provide a backing and to form a key for plaster.

LIERNE RIBS: short subsidiary ribs tieing main ribs in a vault.

LIGHT: the division of a window by mullion and transom; can be further subdivided into panes.

LINENFOLD: panelling carved to look like vertically folded linen.

LINTEL: block of stone spanning top of a doorway or window.

LOGGIA: a covered arcade or colonnade open on at least one side.

LOUVRE(D): a series of inclined and overlapping boards or slats, fixed horizontally to admit air but exclude rain.

MACHICOLATION: a projecting parapet on a castle wall or tower with openings in the floor between the corbels through which missiles could be dropped.

MAGNESIAN LIMESTONE: a limestone of the Permian system, some two hundred million years old where carbonate of magnesium replaced carbonate of calcium. Also referred to as 'dolomitic'.

MANSARD: a roof with two pitches on each side of the ridge, the lower one steeper than the other.

MISERICORD: a bracket on the underside of a hinged wooden seat in a choir stall which afforded support during long periods of standing.

MODILLION: small projecting brackets, often placed in a series below a Classical cornice.

MOULD, MOULDINGS: varieties of contour given to piers, arches etc. *See* CABLE, DOG-TOOTH, DRIPSTONE.

MULLION: a vertical structural member subdividing a window.

NEWEL: central column from which steps of a winding staircase radiate, and also the principal posts at the angles of a square staircase which support the handrail.

NICHE: a shaped recess in a wall or screen.

NOGGING: brickwork used as infilling for half-timbered buildings.

OFFSET: *see* SET-OFF.

OGEE: a continuous double curve, concave above and convex below, or vice versa.

OOLITE: limestone mainly composed of abundant small calcareous grains, resembling the roe of a fish.

ORDERS: the classical styles of columns with combinations of base, shaft, capital and entablature; Doric (Greek, Roman and Tuscan) Ionic and Corinthian.

ORIEL: a window projecting from an upper storey.

OVERHANG: projecting upper storey of a building. *See* JETTY.

OVERTHROW: the fixed panel or arch, often elaborately decorated, above a wrought-iron gate.

PALLADIO, ANDREA: Italian architect (1508–80) whose work was introduced to England by Inigo Jones in 1615. It was revived in the eighteenth century by Colen Campbell and Lord Burlington. Hence 'Palladian'.

PARAPET: a low wall on bridge, castle, church, gallery or balcony, above the cornice.

PARCLOSE: a screen separating a chapel or aisle from the body of the church.

PARGETTING: external plasterwork treated ornamentally, incised or in relief.

PARLATORIUM: parlour, part of monastery where conversation was allowed.

PARTERRE: a flower-garden.

PEDIMENT: in Classical, Renaissance and neo-Classical buildings, a gable of low pitch, straight-sided or curved segmentally, above a door, window or portico.

PELE TOWER: a fortified tower found in the North of England and Scotland.

PERPENDICULAR: period of English Gothic architecture c.1335–1530, characterised by strong vertical tracery.

PIANO NOBILE: the principal storey of a house containing the state rooms; usually the first floor.

PIER: a solid masonry support to sustain vertical pressure; simple – round, square or rectangular, or compound, composite and multi-form, with mouldings and shafts.

PILASTER: a flat pier or shallow projection attached to a wall, with a base and capital.

PINNACLE: an ornament, pyramidical or conical and often decorated which surmounts a gable or buttress.

PISCINA: a recess containing a shallow stone basin, with a drain, for washing sacred vessels, almost always to the south of an altar.

PLINTH: the projecting base of a wall or column, usually moulded or chamfered at the top.

POINTING: filling in the joint-lines of brick and stonework with mortar or cement, smoothed with the point of a trowel.

PORTICO: a covered colonnade providing an entrance to a building.

PULPITUM: solid screen shutting off choir from the nave in a major church and providing, on its eastern side, a backing for the return stalls.

PURLIN: a longitudinal horizontal beam or pole supporting the common rafters of a roof.

QUOIN: a dressed stone at the external angle of a wall.

RAGSTONE: a hard rubbly or coarse shelly stone.

RANDOM: not laid in courses; undressed stone of many shapes and sizes.

RENDERING: covering of an outer wall, with, for example, plaster, or cement and sand.

REREDOS: wall or screen behind an altar, usually ornamented.

RETICULATED TRACERY: tracery of net-like character.

RIB: a length of stone or wood, generally moulded, dividing the compartments of a vault or roof.

RIDGE: the member laid longitudinally at the apex of a timber roof against which the rafters rest.

ROCOCO: a decorative phase in England, c.1720–1760, especially associated with elaborately designed plasterwork, chimney-pieces and furniture.

ROLL: a plain moulding.

ROMANESQUE: style of architecture prevalent in the eleventh and twelfth centuries.

ROOD: a crucifix; the cross usually found in a Rood Loft, a gallery built over the rood screen.

ROTUNDA: circular or oval building, often domed.

ROUNDEL: panel, disc or medallion, circular in shape.

RUBBLE, RUBBLESTONE: unsquared and undressed stone, not laid in regular courses.

RUSTICATION: the practice of surrounding blocks of stone by sunk joints in order to produce shadows.

SACRISTY: a room in or attached to a church where sacred vessels are kept.

SASH: a glazed wooden frame which slides up and down by means of pulleys.

SCALLOPED CAPITAL: where the semi-circular surface of the capital is elaborated into 'scallops' or a series of truncated cones.

SEDILE (PL. SEDILIA): seat or seats, usually three for the clergy on the south side of the chancel.

SET-OFF: a sloped horizontal break on the surface of a wall or buttress, formed where the portion above is reduced in thickness.

SEGMENT, SEGMENTAL: in an arch the segment of a semi-circle drawn from a centre below the springing line.

SHAFT: the main part of a column between base and capital; in Gothic architecture it can also be a small column.

SHINGLES: thin pieces of wood used for covering roofs, walls and spires.

SPANDREL: the space, approximately triangular, between the outer curve of an arch and the rectangle formed by the mouldings enclosing it.

SPROCKET: a short length of timber attached to the face of a rafter a little above the eaves in order to give the lowest part of a roof a flatter pitch.

STIFF-LEAF: foliage of conventional form, with stiff stems and lobed leaves that characterises Early English ornament on mouldings etc.

STRAPWORK: sixteenth- and seventeenth-century flat interlaced decoration, seemingly derived from bands of cut leather.

STRING COURSE: a moulding or narrow projecting course running horizontally along the face of a building.

SWAG: an ornamental wreath or festoon of flowers, foliage or fruit fastened at both ends, and hanging down in the centre.

TEMPIETTO: a small, temple-like structure or shape.

TERRACOTTA: burnt clay, unglazed.

TESTER: flat canopy serving as a sounding-board over a pulpit.

TIE-BEAM: a beam at the base of a roof-truss, spanning the space from wall to wall.

TRACERY: intersecting ornamental ribwork in the upper parts of Gothic windows, walls, screens and vaults.

TRANSEPT: an arm of the cross-piece of a cruciform church.

TRANSOM: a horizontal structural member subdividing a window.

TRIBUNE: a gallery extending over the whole roof of an aisle.

TRIFORIUM: an arcaded wall passage or area of blank arcading above the main arcade of a church and below the clerestory.

TROMPE L'OEIL: a painting giving the illusion that objects represented are real.

TRUSS: a group of strong timbers arranged as a supporting frame within the triangle formed by the sloping sides of a timber-framed roof.

TUMBLING: bricks laid at right-angles to the slope of a roof.

TYMPANUM: the area between the lintel and the arch of a doorway, often filled with relief sculpture.

UNDERCROFT: a vaulted underground room or crypt.

VALLEY: the sloping junction of two inclined roof surfaces.

VAULT: arched roof of stone; *fan-vault* where the length and curvature of the ribs which spring from the same point are similar; a *lierne-vault* incorporates decorative short subsidiary ribs.

VENETIAN WINDOW: a window with three openings, the middle one arched and wider than the others.

VERMICULATION: dressing the surface of a block of stone so that it appears to be covered with worm-tracks.

VESTIBULE: an ante-room or entrance hall or passage.

VOUSSOIR: a wedge-shaped stone for an arch.

WAGON ROOF: a curved wooden rafter roof giving the appearance of the inside of a canvas tilt over a wagon.

WEATHER-BOARDING: boards providing an external covering for a wall-surface, usually fixed horizontally and generally overlapping.

INDEX

The 100 buildings are shown in capitals. Page numbers of photographs are shown in bold type.